YOUR UNITED STATES

[See page 28

THE GLORY OF FIFTH AVENUE INSPIRES EVEN THOSE ON FOOT

YOUR
UNITED STATES

IMPRESSIONS OF A FIRST VISIT

BY
ARNOLD BENNETT

ILLUSTRATED BY
FRANK CRAIG

HARPER & BROTHERS PUBLISHERS
NEW YORK AND LONDON
MCMXII

H-O

CONTENTS

ILLUSTRATIONS

ILLUSTRATIONS

I

THE FIRST NIGHT

YOUR UNITED STATES

I

THE FIRST NIGHT

I SAT with a melting ice on my plate, and my gaze on a very distant swinging door, through which came and went every figure except the familiar figure I desired. The figure of a woman came. She wore a pale-blue dress and a white apron and cap, and carried a dish in uplifted hands, with the gesture of an acolyte. On the bib of the apron were two red marks, and as she approached, tripping, scornful, unheeding, along the interminable carpeted aisle, between serried tables of correct diners, the vague blur of her face gradually developed into features, and the two red marks on her stomacher grew into two rampant lions, each holding a globe in its ferocious paws; and she passed on, bearing away the dish and these mysterious symbols, and lessened into a puppet on the horizon of the enormous hall, and finally vanished through another door. She was succeeded by men, all bearing dishes, but none of them so inexorably scornful as she, and none of them disappearing where she had disappeared; every man relented and stopped at some table or other. But the figure I

3

desired remained invisible, and my ice continued to melt, in accordance with chemical law. The orchestra in the gallery leaped suddenly into the rag-time without whose accompaniment it was impossible, anywhere in the civilized world, to dine correctly. That rag-time, committed, I suppose, originally by some well-intentioned if banal composer in the privacy of his study one night, had spread over the whole universe of restaurants like a pest, to the exasperation of the sensitive, but evidently to the joy of correct diners. Joy shone in the elated eyes of the four hundred persons correctly dining together in this high refectory, and at the end there was honest applause! . . . And yet you never encountered a person who, questioned singly, did not agree and even assert of his own accord that music at meals is an outrageous nuisance! . . .

However, my desired figure was at length manifest. The man came hurrying and a little breathless, with his salver, at once apologetic and triumphant. My ice was half liquid. Had I not the right to reproach him, in the withering, contemptuous tone which correct diners have learned to adopt toward the alien serfs who attend them? I had not. I had neither the right nor the courage nor the wish. This man was as Anglo-Saxon as myself. He had, with all his deference, the mien of the race. When he dreamed of paradise, he probably did not dream of the *caisse* of a cosmopolitan Grand Hotel in Switzerland. When he spoke English he was not speaking a foreign language. And this restaurant was one of the extremely few fashionable Anglo-Saxon restaurants left in the world, where an order given in English is understood at the first try, and where the English language is not assassinated and dismembered by menials who despise it, menials who slang one another openly in the patois of Geneva, Luxembourg, or Naples. A singular survival, this restaurant! . . . Moreover, the man was justified in his triumphant air. Not only had he most intelligently brought me a fresh ice, but he had brought the particular kind of rusk for which I had asked. There were over thirty dishes on the emblazoned menu, and of course I had wanted something that was not on it: a peculiar rusk, a rusk recondite and unheard of by my fellow-diners. The man had hopefully said that he "would see." And here lay the rusk, magically obtained. I felicitated him, as an equal. And then, having consumed the ice and the fruits of the hot-house, I arose and followed in the path of the lion-breasted woman, and arrived at an elevator, and was wafted aloft by a boy of sixteen who did nothing else from 6 A.M. till midnight (so he said) but ascend and descend in that elevator. By the discipline of this inspiring and jocund task he was being prepared for manhood and the greater world! ... And yet, what would you? Elevators must have boys, and even men. Civilization is not so simple as it may seem to the passionate reformer and lover of humanity.

Later, in the vast lounge above the restaurant, I formed one of a group of men, most of whom had acquired fame, and had the slight agreeable self-consciousness that fame gives; and I listened, against a background of the ever-insistent music, to one of those endless and multifarious reminiscent conversations that are heard only in such places. The companion on my right would tell how he had inhabited a house in Siam, next to the temple in front of which the corpses of people too poor to be burned were laid out, after surgical preliminaries, to be devoured by vultures, and how the vultures, when gorged, would flap to the roof of his house and sit there in contemplation. And the companion on my left would tell how, when he was unfamous and on his beam-ends, he would stay in bed with a sham attack of influenza, and on the day when a chance offered itself would get up and don his only suit—a glorious one—and, fitting an eye-glass into his eye because it made him look older, would go forth to confront the chance. And then the talk might be interrupted in order to consult the morning paper, and so settle a dispute about the exact price of Union Pacifics. And then an Italian engineer would tell about sport in the woods of Maine, a perfect menagerie of wild animals where it was advisable to use a revolver lest the excessive noise of a fowling-piece should disturb the entire forest, and how once he had shot seven times at an imperturbable partridge showing its head over a tree, and missed seven times, and how the partridge had at last flown off, with a flicker of plumage that almost said aloud, "Well, I really can't wait any longer!" And then might follow a simply tremendous discussion about the digestibility of buckwheat-cakes.

And then the conversation of every group in the lounge would be stopped by the entry of a page bearing a telegram and calling out in the voice of destiny the name of him to whom the telegram was addressed. And then another companion would relate in intricate detail a recent excursion into Yucatan, speaking negligently—as though it were a trifle—of the extraordinary beauty of the women of Yucatan, and in the end making quite plain his conviction that no other women were as beautiful as the women of Yucatan. And then the inevitable Mona Lisa would get onto the carpet, and one heard, apropos, of the theft of Adam mantelpieces from Russell Square, and of superb masterpieces of paint rotting with damp in neglected Venetian churches, and so on and so on, until one had the melancholy illusion that the whole art world was going or gone to destruction. But this subject did not really hold us, for the reason that, beneath a blasé exterior, we were all secretly preoccupied by the beauty of the women of Yucatan and wondering whether we should ever get to Yucatan. . . . And then, looking by accident away, I saw the dim, provocative faces of girls in white jerseys and woolen caps peering from without through the dark double windows of the lounge. And I was glad when somebody suggested that it was time to take a turn. And outside, in the strong wind, abaft the four funnels of the *Lusitania*, a star seemed to be dancing capriciously around and about the masthead light. And it was difficult to believe that the masthead and its light, and not the star, were dancing.

From the lofty promenade deck the Atlantic wave is a little enough thing, so far down beneath you that you can scarcely even sniff its salty tang. But when the elevator-boy—always waiting for me—had lowered me through five floors, I stood on tiptoe and gazed through the thick glass of a porthole there; and the flying Atlantic wave, theatrically moonlit now, was very near. Suddenly something jumped up and hit the glass of the porthole a fearful, crashing blow that made me draw away my face in alarm; and the solid ground on which I stood vibrated for an instant. It was the Atlantic wave, caressing. Anybody on the other side of this thin, nicely painted steel plate (I thought) would be in a rather hopeless situation. I turned away, half shivering, from the menace. All was calm and warm and reassuring within the ship. . . . In the withdrawn privacy of my berth, with the curtains closed over the door and Murray Gilchrist's new novel in my hand and a poised electric lamp over my head, I looked about as I lay, and everything was still except a towel that moved gently, almost imperceptibly, to and fro. Yet the towel had copied the immobility of the star. It alone did not oscillate. Forty-five thousand tons were swaying; but not that towel. The sense of actual present romance was too strong to let me read. I extinguished the light, and listened in the dark to the faint straining noises of the enormous organism. I thought: "This magic thing is taking me *there!* In three days I shall be on that shore." Terrific adventure! The rest of the passengers were merely going to America.

The magic thing was much more magic than I had conceived. The next morning, being up earlier than usual and wandering about on strange, inclosed decks unfamiliar to my feet, I beheld astonishing unsuspected populations of men and women—crowds of them—a healthy, powerful, prosperous, independent, somewhat stern and disdainful multitude, it seemed to me. Those muscular, striding girls in caps and shawls would not yield an inch to me in their promenade; they brushed strongly and carelessly past me; had I been a ghost they would have walked through me. They were, and had been, all living—eating and sleeping—somewhere within the vessel, and I had not imagined it! It is true that some ass in the saloon had already calculated for my benefit that there were "three thousand *souls* on board!" (The solemn use of the word "souls" in this connection by a passenger should stamp a man forever.) But such numerical statements do not really arouse the imagination. I had to see with my eyes. And I did see with my eyes. That afternoon a high officer of the ship, spiriting me away from the polite flirtations and pastimes of the upper decks, carried me down to more exciting scenes. And I saw a whole string of young women inoculated against smallpox, under the interested gaze of a crowd of men ranged on a convenient staircase. And a little later I saw a whole string of men inoculated against smallpox, under the interested gaze of a crowd of young women ranged on a convenient staircase.

"They're having their sweet revenge," said the high officer, indicating the young women. He was an epigrammatic and terse speaker. When I reflected aloud upon the order and discipline of service which was necessary to maintain more than a thousand roughish persons in idleness, cleanliness, health, peace, and content, in the inelastic forward spaces of the ship, he said with a certain grimness: "Everything has to be screwed up as tight as you can screw it. And you must keep to the round. What you do to-day you must do to-morrow. But what you don't do to-day you can't get done to-morrow."

Nevertheless, it proved to be a very human world, a world in which the personal equation counted. I remember that while some four hundred in one long hall were applauding "Home, Sweet Home," very badly fiddled by a gay man on a stool ("Home, Sweet Home" —and half of them Scandinavians!), and another four hundred or so were sitting expectant on those multifarious convenient staircases or wandering in and out of the maze of cubicles that contained fifteen hundred separate berths, and a third four hundred or so in another long hall were consuming a huge tea offered to them by a cohort of stewards in white—I remember that while all this was going forward and the complex mechanism of the kitchen was in full strain a little, untidy woman, with an infant dragging at one hand and a mug in the other, strolled nonchalantly into the breathless kitchen, and said to a hot cook, "Please will you give me a drop o' milk for this child?" And under the military gaze of the high officer, too! Something awful should have happened. The engines ought to have stopped. The woman ought to have been ordered out to instant execution. The engines did seem to falter for a moment. But the high officer grimly smiled, and they went on again. "Give me yer mug, mother," said the cook. And the untidy woman went off with her booty.

"Now I'll show you the first-class kitchens," the high officer said, and guided me through uncharted territories to chambers where spits were revolving in front of in-

DISEMBARKING AT NEW YORK

tense heat, and where a confectionery business proceeded, night and day, and dough was mixed by electricity, and potatoes peeled by the same, and where a piece of clock-work lifted an egg out of boiling water after it had lain therein the number of seconds prescribed by you. And there, pinned to a board, was the order I had given for a special dinner that night. And there, too, more impressive even than that order, was a list of the several hundred stewards, together with a designation of the post of each in case of casualty. I noticed that thirty or forty of them were told off "to control passengers." After all, we were in the midst of the Atlantic, and in a crisis the elevator-boys themselves would have more authority than any passenger, however gorgeous. A thought salutary for gorgeous passengers—that they were in the final resort mere fool bodies to be controlled! After I had seen the countless store-rooms, in the recesses of each of which was hidden a clerk with a pen behind his ear and a nervous and taciturn air, and passed on to the world of the second cabin, which was a surprisingly brilliant imitation of the great world of the saloon, I found that I held a much-diminished opinion of the great world of the saloon, which I now perceived to be naught but a thin crust or artificial gewgaw stuck over the truly thrilling parts of the ship.

It was not, however, till the next day that I realized what the most thrilling part of the ship was. Under the protection of another high officer I had climbed to the bridge—seventy-five feet above the level of the sea—which bridge had been very seriously disestablished by an ambitious wave a couple of years before—and had there inspected the devices for detecting and extinguishing fires in distant holds by merely turning a handle, and the charts and the telephones and the telegraphs, and the under-water signaling, and the sounding-tubes, and the officers' piano; and I had descended by way of the capstan-gear (which, being capable of snapping a chain that would hold two hundred and sixty tons in suspension, was suitably imprisoned in a cage, like a fierce wild animal) right through the length of the vessel to the wheel-house aft. It was comforting to know that if six alternative steering-wheels were smashed, one after another, there remained a seventh gear to be worked, chiefly by direct force of human arm. And, after descending several more stories, I had seen the actual steering — the tremendous affair moving to and fro, majestic and apparently capricious, in obedience to the light touch of a sailor six hundred feet distant. And then I had seen the four shafts, revolving lazily one hundred and eighty-four to the minute; and got myself involved in dangerous forests of greasy machinery, whizzing all deserted in a very high temperature under electric bulbs. Only at rare intervals did I come across a man in brown doing nothing in particular—as often as not gazing at a dial; there were dials everywhere, showing pressures and speeds. And then I had come to the dynamo-room, where the revolutions were twelve hundred to the minute, and then to the turbines themselves—insignificant little things, with no swagger of huge crank and piston, disappointing little things that developed as much as one-third of the horse-power required for all the electricity of New York.

THE FIRST NIGHT

And then, lastly, when I had supposed myself to be at the rock-bottom of the steamer, I had been instructed to descend in earnest, and I went down and down steel ladders, and emerged into an enormous, an incredible cavern, where a hundred and ninety gigantic furnaces were being fed every ten minutes by hundreds of tiny black dolls called firemen. I, too, was a doll as I looked up at the high white-hot mouth of a furnace and along the endless vista of mouths. . . . Imagine hell with the addition of electric light, and you have it! . . . And upstairs, far above on the surface of the water, confectioners were making fancy cakes, and the elevator-boy was doing his work! . . . Yes, the inferno was the most thrilling part of the ship; and no other part of the ship could hold a candle to it. And I remained of this conviction even when I sat in the captain's own room, smoking his august cigars and turning over his books. I no longer thought, "Every revolution of the propellers brings me nearer to that shore." I thought, "Every shovelful flung into those white - hot mouths brings me nearer."

It is an absolute fact that, four hours before we could hope to disembark, ladies in mantles and shore hats (seeming fantastic and enormous after the sobriety of ship attire), and gentlemen in shore hats and dark overcoats, were standing in attitudes of expectancy in the saloon-hall, holding wraps and small bags: some of their faces had never been seen till then in the public resorts of the ship. Excitement will indeed take strange forms. For myself, although I was on the threshold

13

of the greatest adventure of my life, I was unaware of being excited—I had not even "smelled" land, to say nothing of having seen it—until, when it was quite dark, I descried a queerly arranged group of different-colored lights in the distance—yellow, red, green, and what not. My thoughts ran instantly to Coney Island. I knew that Coney was an island, and that it was a place where people had to be attracted and distracted somehow, and I decided that these illuminations were a device of the pleasure-mongers of Coney. And when the ship began to salute these illuminations with answering flares I thought the captain was a rather good-natured man to consent thus to amuse the populace. But when we slowed, our propellers covering the calm sea with acres of foam, and the whole entire illuminations began to approach us in a body, I perceived that my Coney Island was merely another craft, but a very important and official craft. An extremely small boat soon detached itself from this pyrotechnical craft and came with a most extraordinary leisureness toward a white square of light that had somehow broken forth in the blackness of our side. And looking down from the topmost deck, I saw, far below, the tiny boat manœuver on the glinting wave into the reflection of our electricity and three mysterious men climb up from her and disappear into us. Then it was that I grew really excited, uncomfortably excited. The United States had stretched out a tentacle.

In no time at all, as it seemed, another and more formidable tentacle had folded round me—in the shape of two interviewers. (How these men had got on board

—and how my own particular friend had got on board
—I knew not, for we were yet far from quay-side.) I
had been hearing all my life about the sublime American
institution of the interview. I had been warned by
Americans of its piquant dangers. And here I was suddenly up against it! Beneath a casual and jaunty exterior, I trembled. I wanted to sit, but dared not.
They stood; I stood. These two men, however, were
adepts. They had the better qualities of American
dentists. Obviously they spent their lives in meeting
notorieties on inbound steamers, and made naught of it.
They were middle-aged, disillusioned, tepidly polite,
conscientious, and rapid. They knew precisely what
they wanted and how to get it. Having got it, they
raised their hats and went. Their printed stories were
brief, quite unpretentious, and inoffensive—though one
of them did let out that the most salient part of me was
my teeth, and the other did assert that I behaved
like a school-boy. (Doubtless the result of timidity
trying to be dignified—this alleged school-boyishness!)

I liked these men. But they gave me an incomplete
idea of the race of interviewers in the United States.
There is a variety of interviewers very different from
them. I am, I think, entitled to consider myself a fairly
first-class authority on all varieties of interviewer, not
only in New York but in sundry other great cities. My
initiation was brief, but it was thorough. Many varieties won my regard immediately, and kept it; but
I am conscious that my sympathy with one particular
brand (perhaps not numerous) was at times imperfect.
The brand in question, as to which I was amiably

15

cautioned before even leaving the steamer, is usually very young, and as often a girl as a youth. He or she cheerfully introduces himself or herself with a hint that of course it is an awful bore to be interviewed, but he or she has a job to do and he or she must be allowed to do it. Just so! But the point which, in my audacity, I have occasionally permitted to occur to me is this: Is this sort of interviewer capable of doing the job allotted to him? I do not mind slips of reporting, I do not mind a certain agreeable malice (indeed, I reckon to do a bit in that line myself). I do not even mind hasty misrepresentations (for, after all, we are human, and the millennium is still unannounced); but I do object to inefficiency—especially in America, where sundry kinds of efficiency have been carried farther than any efficiency was ever carried before.

Now this sort of interviewer too often prefaces the operation itself by the remark that he really doesn't know what question to ask you. (Too often I have been tempted to say: "Why not ask me to write the interview for you? It will save you trouble.") Having made this remark, the interviewer usually proceeds to give a sketch of her own career, together with a conspectus of her opinions on everything, a reference to her importance in the interviewing world, and some glimpse of the amount of her earnings. This achieved, she breaks off breathless and reproaches you: "But, my dear man, you aren't saying anything at all. You really must say something." ("My dear man" is the favorite form of address of this sort of interviewer when she happens to be a girl.) Too often I have been tempted

THE DOWN-TOWN BROADWAY OF CROWDED SKY-SCRAPERS

to reply: "Cleopatra, or Helen, which of us is being interviewed?" When he has given you a chance to talk, this sort of interviewer listens, helps, corrects, advises, but never makes a note. The result the next morning is the anticipated result. The average newspaper reader gathers that an extremely brilliant young man or woman has held converse with a very commonplace stranger who, being confused in his or her presence, committed a number of absurdities which offered a strong and painful contrast to the cleverness and wisdom of the brilliant youth. This result apparently satisfies the average newspaper reader, but it does not satisfy the expert.

Immediately after my first bout with interviewers I was seated at a table in the dining-saloon of the ship with my particular friend and three or four friendly, quiet, modest, rather diffident human beings whom I afterward discovered to be among the best and most experienced newspaper men in New York—not interviewers.

Said one of them:

"Not every interviewer in New York knows how to *write*—how to put a sentence together decently. And there are perhaps a few who don't accurately know the difference between impudence and wit."

A caustic remark, perhaps. But I have noticed that when the variety of interviewing upon which I have just animadverted becomes the topic, quiet, reasonable Americans are apt to drop into causticity.

Said another:

"I was a reporter for twelve years, but I was cured of personalities at an early stage—and by a nigger, too!

I had been interviewing a nigger prize-fighter, and I'd made some remarks about the facial characteristics of niggers in general. Some other nigger wrote me a long letter of protest, and it ended like this: 'I've never seen you. But I've seen your portraits, and let me respectfully tell you that *you're* no Lillian Russell.'"

Some mornings I, too, might have sat down and written, from visual observation, "Let me respectfully tell you that *you're* no Lillian Russell."

Said a third among my companions:

"No importance whatever is attached to a certain kind of interview in the United States."

Which I found, later, was quite true in theory, but not in practice. Whenever, in that kind of interview, I had been made to say something more acutely absurd and maladroit than usual, my friends who watched over me, and to whom I owe so much that cannot be written, were a little agitated—for about half an hour; in about half an hour the matter had somehow passed from their minds.

"Supposing I refuse to talk to that sort of interviewer?" I asked, at the saloon table.

"The interviews will appear all the same," was the reply.

My subsequent experience contradicted this. On the rare occasions when I refused to be interviewed, what appeared was not an interview, but .invective.

Let me not be misunderstood. I have been speaking of only one brand of American interviewer. I encountered a couple of really admirable women interviewers, not too young, and a confraternity of men who did not disdain an elementary knowledge of their business. One of these arrived with a written list of questions, took a shorthand note of all I said, and then brought me a proof to correct. In interviewing this amounts almost to genius. . . . I have indicated what to me seems a defect—trifling, possibly, but still a defect—in the brilliant organization of the great national sport of interviewing. Were this defect removed, as it could be, the institution might be as perfect as the American oyster. Than which nothing is more perfect.

"You aren't drinking your coffee," said some one, inspecting my cup at the saloon table.

"No," I answered, firmly; for when the smooth efficiency of my human machine is menaced I am as faddy and nervous as a marine engineer over lubrication. "If I did, I shouldn't sleep."

"And what of it?" demanded my particular friend, challengingly.

It was a rebuke. It was as if he had said, "On this great night, when you enter my wondrous and romantic country for the first time, what does it matter whether you sleep or not?"

I saw the point. I drank the coffee. The romantic sense, which had been momentarily driven back by the discussion of general ideas, swept over me again. . . . In fact, through the saloon windows could be seen all the Battery end of New York and the first vague visions of sky-scrapers. . . . Then—the moments refused to be counted—we were descending by lifts and by gangways from the high upper decks of the ship down onto the rocky ground of the United States. I don't think that any American ever set foot in Europe with a more profound and delicious thrill than that which affected me at that instant. . . . I was there! . . . The official and unofficial activities of the quay passed before me like a dream. . . . I heard my name shouted by a man in a formidably severe uniform, and I thought, "Thus early have I somehow violated the Constitution of these States?" But it was only a telegram for me. . . . And then I was in a most rickety and confined taxi, and the taxi was full to the brim with luggage, two friends, and me. And I was off into New York.

At the center of the first cross-roads I saw a splendid and erect individual, flashing forth authority, gaiety, and utter smartness in the gloom. Impossible not to believe that he was the owner of all the adjacent ground, disguised as a cavalry officer on foot.

"What is that archduke?" I inquired.

"He's just a cop."

I knew then that I was in a great city.

The rest of the ride was an enfevered phantasmagoria. We burst startlingly into a very remarkable deep glade —on the floor of it long and violent surface-cars, a few open shops and bars with commissionaires at the doors, vehicles dipping and rising out of holes in the ground, vistas of forests of iron pillars, on the top of which ran deafening, glittering trains, as on a tight-rope; above all that, a layer of darkness; and above the layer of darkness enormous moving images of things in electricity —a mastodon kitten playing with a ball of thread, an umbrella in a shower of rain, siphons of soda-water

BROADWAY ON ELECTION NIGHT

being emptied and filled, gigantic horses galloping at full speed, and an incredible heraldry of chewing-gum. . . . Sky-signs! In Europe I had always inveighed manfully against sky-signs. But now I bowed the head, vanquished. These sky-signs annihilated argument. Moreover, had they not been made possible by the invention of a European, and that European an intimate friend of my own? . . .

"I suppose this is Broadway?" I ventured.

It was. That is to say, it was one of the Broadways. There are several different ones. What could be more different from this than the down-town Broadway of Trinity Church and the crowded sky-scrapers? And even this Broadway could differ from itself, as I knew later on an election night. . . . I was overpowered by Broadway.

"You must not expect me to talk," I said.

We drew up in front of a huge hotel and went into the bar, huge and gorgeous to match, shimmering with white bartenders and a variegated population of men-about-town. I had never seen such a bar.

"Two Polands and a Scotch highball," was the order. Of which geographical language I understood not a word.

"See the fresco," my particular friend suggested. And from his tone, at once modestly content and artificially careless, I knew that that nursery-rhyme fresco was one of the sights of the pleasure quarter of New York, and that I ought to admire it. Well, I did admire it. I found it rather fine and apposite. But the free-luncheon counter, as a sight, took my fancy more. Here it was,

the free-luncheon counter of which the European reads
—generously loaded, and much freer than the air.

"Have something?"

I would not. They could shame me into drinking
coffee, but they could not shame me into eating corned
beef and granite biscuits at eleven o'clock at night.
The Poland water sufficed me.

We swept perilously off again into the welter. That
same evening three of my steamer companions were
thrown out of a rickety taxi into a hole in the ground
in the middle of New York, with the result that one of
them spent a week in a hotel bed, under doctor and nurse.
But I went scatheless. Such are the hazards of life. . . .
We arrived at a terminus. And it was a great terminus.
A great terminus is an inhospitable place. And just
here, in the perfection of the manner in which my
minutest comfort was studied and provided for, I began
to appreciate the significance of American hospitality—
that combination of eager good-nature, Oriental lavishness, and sheer brains. We had time to spare. Close
to the terminus we had passed by a hotel whose summit,
for all my straining out of the window of the cab, I had
been unable to descry. I said that I should really like
to see the top of that hotel. No sooner said than done.
I saw the highest hotel I had ever seen. We went into
the hotel, teeming like the other one, and from an agreeable and lively young dandy bought three cigars out of
millions of cigars. Naught but bank-notes seemed to
be current. The European has an awe of bank-notes,
whatever their value.

Then we were in the train, and the train was moving.

THE FIRST NIGHT

And every few seconds it shot past the end of a long, straight, lighted thoroughfare—scores upon scores of them, with a wider and more brilliant street interspersed among them at intervals. And I forgot at what hundredth street the train paused before rolling finally out of New York. I had had the feeling of a vast and metropolitan city. I thought, "Whatever this is or is not, it is a metropolis, and will rank with the best of 'em." I had lived long in more than one metropolis, and I knew the proud and the shameful unmistakable marks of the real thing. And I was aware of a poignant sympathy with those people and those mysterious generations who had been gradually and yet so rapidly putting together, girder by girder and tradition by tradition, all unseen by me till then, this illustrious, proud organism, with its nobility and its baseness, its rectitude and its mournful errors, its colossal sense of life. I liked New York irrevocably.

II

STREETS

II

WHEN I first looked at Fifth Avenue by sunlight, in the tranquillity of Sunday morning, and when I last set eyes on it, in the ordinary peevish gloom of a busy sailing-day, I thought it was the proudest thoroughfare I had ever seen anywhere. The revisitation of certain European capitals has forced me to modify this judgment; but I still think that Fifth Avenue, if not unequaled, is unsurpassed.

One afternoon I was driving up Fifth Avenue in the company of an architectural expert who, with the incredible elastic good nature of American business men, had abandoned his affairs for half a day in order to go with me on a voyage of discovery, and he asked me, so as to get some basis of understanding or disagreement, what building in New York had pleased me most. I at once said the University Club—to my mind a masterpiece. He approved, and a great peace filled our automobile; in which peace we expanded. He asked me what building in the world made the strongest appeal to me, and I at once said the Strozzi Palace at Florence. Whereat he was decidedly sympathetic.

"Fifth Avenue," I said, "always reminds me of Florence and the Strozzi. . . . The cornices, you know."

He stopped the automobile under the Gorham store

and displayed to me the finest cornice in New York, and told me how Stanford White had put up several experimental cornices there before arriving at finality. Indeed, a great cornice! I admit I was somewhat dashed by the information that most cornices in New York are made of cast iron; but only for a moment! What, after all, do I care what a cornice is made of, so long as it juts proudly out from the façade and helps the street to a splendid and formidable sky-line? I had neither read nor heard a word of the cornices of New York, and yet for me New York was first and last the city of effective cornices! (Which merely shows how eyes differ!) The cornice must remind you of Italy, and through Italy of the Renaissance. And is it not the boast of the United States to be a renaissance? I always felt that there was something obscurely symbolic in the New York cornice—symbolic of the necessary qualities of a renaissance, half cruel and half humane.

The critical European excusably expects a very great deal from Fifth Avenue, as being the principal shopping street of the richest community in the world. (I speak not of the residential blocks north of Fifty-ninth Street, whose beauty and interest fall perhaps far short of their pretensions.) And the critical European will not be disappointed, unless his foible is to be disappointed—as, in fact, occasionally happens. Except for the miserly splitting, here and there in the older edifices, of an inadequate ground floor into a mezzanine and a shallow box (a device employed more frankly and usefully with an outer flight of steps on the East Side), there is nothing mean in the whole street from the Plaza to Wash-

28

ington Square. A lot of utterly mediocre architecture there is, of course—the same applies inevitably to every long street in every capital—but the general effect is homogeneous and fine, and, above all, grandly generous. And the alternation of high and low buildings produces not infrequently the most agreeable architectural accidents: for example, seen from about Thirtieth Street, the pale-pillared, squat structure of the Knickerbocker Trust against a background of the lofty red of the Æolian Building. . . . And then, that great white store on the opposite pavement! The single shops, as well as the general stores and hotels on Fifth Avenue, are impressive in the lavish spaciousness of their disposition. Neither stores nor shops could have been conceived, or could be kept, by merchants without genuine imagination and faith.

And the glory of the thoroughfare inspires even those who only walk up and down it. It inspires particularly the mounted policeman as he reigns over a turbulent crossing. It inspires the women, and particularly the young women, as they pass in front of the windows, owning their contents in thought. I sat once with an old, white-haired, and serious gentleman, gazing through glass at Fifth Avenue, and I ventured to say to him, "There are fine women on Fifth Avenue." "By Jove!" he exclaimed, with deep conviction, and his eyes suddenly fired, "there are!" On the whole, I think that, in their carriages or on their feet, they know a little better how to do justice to a fine thoroughfare than the women of any other capital in my acquaintance. I have driven rapidly in a fast car, clinging to my hat and my hair against the New York wind, from one end of Fifth Avenue to the other, and what with the sunshine, and the flags wildly waving in the sunshine, and the blue sky and the cornices jutting into it and the roofs scraping it, and the large whiteness of the stores, and the invitation of the signs, and the display of the windows, and the swift sinuousness of the other cars, and the proud opposing processions of American subjects—what with all this and with the supreme imperialism of the mounted policeman, I have been positively intoxicated!

And yet possibly the greatest moment in the life of Fifth Avenue is at dusk, when dusk falls at tea-time. The street lamps flicker into a steady, steely blue, and the windows of the hotels and restaurants throw a yellow radiance; all the shops—especially the jewelers' shops—become enchanted treasure-houses, whose interiors recede away behind their façades into infinity; and the endless files of innumerable vehicles, interlacing and swerving, put forth each a pair of glittering eyes. . . . Come suddenly upon it all, from the leafy fastnesses of Central Park, round the corner from the Plaza Hotel, and wait your turn until the arm of the policeman, whose blue coat is now whitened with dust, permits your restive chauffeur to plunge down into the main currents of the city. . . . You will have then the most grandiose impression that New York is, in fact, inhabited; and that even though the spectacular luxury of New York be nearly as much founded upon social injustice and poverty as any imperfect human civilization in Europe, it is a boon to be alive therein! . . . In half an hour, in three-quarters of an hour, the vitality is clean gone out of the street. The shops have let down their rich gathered curtains, the pavements are deserted, and the roadway is no longer perilous. And nothing save a fire will arouse Fifth Avenue till the next morning. Even on an election night the sole sign in Fifth Avenue of the disorder of politics will be a few long strips of tape-paper wreathing in the breeze on the asphalt under the lonely lamps.

It is not easy for a visiting stranger in New York to get away from Fifth Avenue. The street seems to hold him fast. There might almost as well be no other avenues; and certainly the word "Fifth" has lost all its numerical significance in current usage. A youthful musical student, upon being asked how many symphonies Beethoven had composed, replied four, and obstinately stuck to it that Beethoven had only composed four. Called upon to enumerate the four, he answered thus, the C minor, the Eroica, the Pastoral, and the Ninth. "Ninth" had lost its numerical significance for that student. A similar phenomenon of psychology has happened with the streets and avenues of New York. Europeans are apt to assume that to tack numbers instead of names on to the thoroughfares of a city is to impair their identities and individualities. Not a bit! The numbers grow into names. That is all. Such is the mysterious poetic force of the human mind! That curt word "Fifth" signifies as much to the New-Yorker as "Boulevard des Italiens" to the Parisian. As for the possibility of confusion, would any New-Yorker ever confuse Fourteenth with Thirteenth or Fifteenth Street, or Twenty-third with Twenty-second or Twenty-fourth, or Forty-second with One Hundred and Forty-second, or One Hundred and Twenty-fifth with anything else whatever? Yes, when the Parisian confuses the Champs Élysées with the Avenue de l'Opéra! When the Parisian arrives at this stage—even then Fifth Avenue will not be confused with Sixth!

One day, in the unusual silence of an election morning, I absolutely determined to see something of the New York that lies beyond Fifth Avenue, and I slipped off westward along Thirty-fourth Street, feeling adventurous. The excursion was indeed an adventure. I came across Broadway and Sixth Avenue together! Sixth Avenue, with its barbaric paving, surely could not be under the same administration as Fifth! Between Sixth and Seventh I met a sinister but genial ruffian, proudly wearing the insignia of Tammany; and soon I met a lot more of them: jolly fellows, apparently, yet somehow conveying to me the suspicion that in a saloon shindy they might prove themselves my superiors. (I was told in New York, and by the best people in New York, that Tammany was a blot on the social system of the city. But I would not have it so. I would call it a part of the social system, just as much a part of the social system, and just as expressive of the national character, as the fine schools, the fine hospitals, the superlative business organizations, or Mr. George M. Cohan's Theater. A civilization is indivisibly responsible for itself. It may not, on the Day of Jugdment, or any other day, lessen its collective responsibility by baptizing certain portions of its organism as extraneous "blots" dropped thereon from without.) To continue—after Seventh

Avenue the declension was frank. In the purlieus of the
Five Towns themselves—compared with which Pitts-
burg is seemingly Paradise—I have never trod such
horrific sidewalks. I discovered huge freight-trains
shunting all over Tenth and Eleventh Avenues, and
frail flying bridges erected from sidewalk to sidewalk,
for the convenience of a brave and hardy populace.
I was surrounded in the street by menacing locomotives
and crowds of Italians, and in front of me was a great
Italian steamer. I felt as though Fifth Avenue was a
three days' journey away, through a hostile country.
And yet I had been walking only twenty minutes! I
regained Fifth with relief, and had learned a lesson. In
future, if asked how many avenues there are in New York
I would insist that there are three: Lexington, Madison,
and Fifth.

The chief characteristic of Broadway is its inter-
minability. Everybody knows, roughly, where it be-
gins, but I doubt if even the topographical experts of
Albany know just where it ends. It is a street that
inspires respect rather than enthusiasm. In the day-
time all the uptown portion of it—and as far down-
town as Ninth Street—has a provincial aspect. If
Fifth Avenue is metropolitan and exclusive, Broadway
is not. Broadway lacks distinction, it lacks any sort
of impressiveness, save in its first two miles, which do—
especially the southern mile—strike you with a vague
and uneasy awe. And it was here that I experienced
my keenest disappointment in the United States.

I went through sundry disappointments. I had expected to be often asked how much I earned. I never was asked. I had expected to be often informed by casual acquaintances of their exact income. Nobody, save an interviewer or so and the president of a great trust, ever passed me even a hint as to the amount of his income. I had expected to find an inordinate amount of tippling in clubs and hotels. I found, on the contrary, a very marked sobriety. I had expected to receive many hard words and some insolence from paid servants, such as train-men, tram-men, lift-boys, and policemen. From this class, as from the others, I received nothing but politeness, except in one instance. That instance, by the way, was a barber in an important hotel, whom I had most respectfully requested to refrain from bumping my head about. "Why?" he demanded. "Because I've got a headache," I said. "Then why didn't you tell me at first?" he crushed me. "Did you expect me to be a thought-reader?" But, indeed, I could say a lot about American barbers. I had expected to have my tempting fob snatched. It was not snatched. I had expected to be asked, at the moment of landing, for my mature opinion of the United States, and again at intervals of about a quarter of an hour, day and night, throughout my stay. But I had been in America at least ten days before the question was put to me, even in jest. I had expected to be surrounded by boasting and impatient vanity concerning the achievements of the United States and the citizens thereof. I literally never heard a word of national boasting, nor observed the slightest impatience under criticism. . . . I say I had expected these things. I would be more

34

A BUSY DAY ON THE CURB MARKET

STREETS

correct to say that I *should* have expected them if
I had had a rumor-believing mind: which I have
not.

But I really did expect to witness an overwhelming
violence of traffic and movement in lower Broadway
and the renowned business streets in its vicinity. And I
really was disappointed by the ordinariness of the scene,
which could be well matched in half a dozen places in
Europe, and beaten in one or two. If but once I had
been shoved into the gutter by a heedless throng going
furiously upon its financial ways, I should have been
content. . . . The legendary "American rush" is to me a
fable. Whether it ever existed I know not; but I certainly saw no trace of it, either in New York or Chicago.
I dare say I ought to have gone to Seattle for it. My
first sight of a stock-market roped off in the street
was an acute disillusionment. In agitation it could not
have competed with a sheep-market. In noise it was a
muffled silence compared with the fine racket that en-
livens the air outside the Paris Bourse. I saw also an
ordinary day in the Stock Exchange. Faint excitations
were afloat in certain corners, but I honestly deemed the
affair tame. A vast litter of paper on the floor, a vast
assemblage of hats pitched on the tops of telephone-
boxes—these phenomena do not amount to a hustle.
Earnest students of hustle should visit Paris or Milan.
The fact probably is that the perfecting of mechanical
contrivances in the United States has killed hustle as
a diversion for the eyes and ears. The mechanical
side of the Exchange was wonderful and delightful.

35

The sky-scrapers that cluster about the lower end of Broadway—their natural home—were as impressive as I could have desired, but not architecturally. For they could only be felt, not seen. And even in situations where the sky-scraper is properly visible, it is, as a rule, to my mind, architecturally a failure. I regret for my own sake that I could not be more sympathetic toward the existing sky-scraper as an architectural entity, because I had assuredly no Europen prejudice against the sky-scraper as such. The objection of most people to the sky-scraper is merely that it is unusual—the instinctive objection of most people to everything that is original enough to violate tradition! I, on the contrary, as a convinced modernist, would applaud the unusualness of the sky-scraper. Nevertheless, I cannot possibly share the feelings of patriotic New-Yorkers who discover architectural grandeur in, say, the Flat Iron Building or the Metropolitan Life Insurance Building. To me they confuse the poetical idea of these buildings with the buildings themselves. I eagerly admit that the bold, prow-like notion of the Flat Iron cutting northward is a splendid notion, an inspiring notion; it thrills. But the building itself is ugly—nay, it is adverbially ugly; and no reading of poetry *into* it will make it otherwise.

Similarly, the Metropolitan Building is tremendous. It is a grand sight, but it is an ugly sight. The men who thought of it, who first conceived the notion of it, were poets. They said, "We will cause to be constructed the highest building in the world; we will bring into existence the most amazing advertisement that an insurance

A WELL-KNOWN WALL STREET CHARACTER

company ever had." That is good; it is superb; it is a proof of heroic imagination. But the actual designers of the building did not rise to the height of it; and if any poetry is left in it, it is not their fault. Think what McKim might have accomplished on that site, and in those dimensions!

Certain architects, feeling the lack of imagination in the execution of these enormous buildings, have set their imagination to work, but in a perverse way and without candidly recognizing the conditions imposed upon them by the sky-scraper form: and the result here and there has been worse than dull; it has been distressing. But here and there, too, one sees the evidence of real understanding and taste. If every tenant of a sky-scraper demands—as I am informed he does—the same windows, and radiators under every window, then the architect had better begin by accepting that demand openly, with no fanciful or pseudo-imaginative pretense that things are not what they are. The Ashland Building, on Fourth Avenue, where the architectural imagination has exercised itself soberly, honestly, and obediently, appeared to me to be a satisfactory and agreeable sky-scraper; and it does not stand alone as the promise that a new style will ultimately be evolved.

In any case, a great deal of the poetry of New York is due to the sky-scraper. At dusk the effect of the massed sky-scrapers illuminated from within, as seen from any high building up-town, is prodigiously beautiful, and it is unique in the cities of this world. The early night effect of the whole town, topped by the aforesaid Metropolitan tower, seen from the New Jersey

shore, is stupendous, and resembles some enchanted
city of the next world rather than of this. And the fact
that a very prominent item in the perspective is a fiery
representation of a frothing glass of beer inconceivably
large—well, this fact too has its importance.

But in the sky-scrapers there is a deeper romanticism
than that which disengages itself from them externally.
You must enter them in order to appreciate them, in
order to respond fully to their complex appeal. Outside, they often have the air of being nothing in particular; at best the façade is far too modest in its revela-
tion of the interior. You can quite easily walk by a
sky-scraper on Broadway without noticing it. But you
cannot actually go into the least of them and not be
impressed. You are in a palace. You are among
marbles and porphyries. You breathe easily in vast
and brilliant foyers that never see daylight. And then
you come to those mysterious palisaded shafts with
which the building and every other building in New
York is secretly honeycombed, and the palisade is opened
and an elevator snatches you up. I think of American
cities as enormous agglomerations in whose inmost dark
recesses innumerable elevators are constantly ascending
and descending, like the angels of the ladder. . . .

The elevator ejects you. You are taken into dazzling
daylight, into what is modestly called a business office;
but it resembles in its grandeur no European business
office, save such as may have been built by an American.
You look forth from a window, and lo! New York and
the Hudson are beneath you, and you are in the skies.
And in the warmed stillness of the room you hear the

THE SKY-SCRAPERS OF LOWER NEW YORK AT NIGHT

wind raging and whistling, as you would have imagined
it could only rage and whistle in the rigging of a three-
master at sea. There are, however, a dozen more stories
above this story. You walk from chamber to chamber,
and in answer to inquiry learn that the rent of this one
suite—among so many—is over thirty-six thousand
dollars a year! And you reflect that, to the beholder
in the street, all that is represented by one narrow row
of windows, lost in a diminishing chess-board of windows.
And you begin to realize what a sky-scraper is, and the
poetry of it.

More romantic even than the sky-scraper finished
and occupied is the sky-scraper in process of construction. From no mean height, listening to the sweet drawl
of the steam-drill, I have watched artisans like dwarfs
at work still higher, among knitted steel, seen them
balance themselves nonchalantly astride girders swinging in space, seen them throwing rivets to one another
and never missing one; seen also a huge crane collapse
under an undue strain, and, crumpling like tinfoil,
carelessly drop its load onto the populous sidewalk
below. That particular mishap obviously raised the
fear of death among a considerable number of people,
but perhaps only for a moment. Anybody in America
will tell you without a tremor (but with pride) that each
story of a sky-scraper means a life sacrificed. Twenty
stories—twenty men snuffed out; thirty stories—thirty
men. A building of some sixty stories is now going up
—sixty corpses, sixty funerals, sixty domestic hearths to
be slowly rearranged, and the registrars alone know how
many widows, orphans, and other loose by-products!

And this mortality, I believe, takes no account of the long battles that are sometimes fought, but never yet to a finish, in the steel webs of those upper floors when the labor-unions have a fit of objecting more violently than usual to non-union labor. In one celebrated building, I heard, the non-unionists contracted an unfortunate habit of getting crippled; and three of them were indiscreet enough to put themselves under a falling girder that killed them, while two witnesses who were ready to give certain testimony in regard to the mishap vanished completely out of the world, and have never since been heard of. And so on. What more natural than that the employers should form a private association for bringing to a close these interesting hazards? You may see the leading spirit of the association. You may walk along the street with him. He knows he is shadowed, and he is quite cheerful about it. His revolver is always very ready for an emergency. Nobody seems to regard this state of affairs as odd enough for any prolonged comment. There it is! It is accepted. It is part of the American dailiness. Nobody, at any rate in the comfortable clubs, seems even to consider that the original cause of the warfare is aught but a homicidal cussedness on the part of the unions. . . . I say that these accidents and these guerrillas mysteriously and grimly proceeding in the skyey fabric of metal-ribbed constructions, do really form part of the poetry of life in America—or should it be the poetry of death? Assuredly they are a spectacular illustration of that sublime, romantic contempt for law and for human life which, to a European, is the most disconcerting factor in the social evolution of your States. I have sat and listened to tales from journalists and other learned connoisseurs till— But enough!

When I left New York and went to Washington I was congratulated on having quitted the false America for the real. When I came to Boston I received the sympathies of everybody in Boston on having been put off for so long with spurious imitations of America, and a sigh of happy relief went up that I had at length got into touch with a genuine American city. When, after a long pilgrimage, I attained Chicago, I was positively informed that Chicago alone was the gate of the United States, and that everything east of Chicago was negligible and even misleading. And when I entered Indianapolis I discovered that Chicago was a mushroom and a suburb of Warsaw, and that its pretension to represent the United States was grotesque, the authentic center of the United States being obviously Indianapolis. . . . The great towns love thus to affront one another, and their demeanor in the game resembles the gamboling of young tigers—it is half playful and half ferocious. For myself, I have to say that my heart was large enough to hold all I saw. While I admit that Indianapolis struck me as very characteristically American, I assert that the unreality of New York escaped me. It appeared to me that New York was quite a real city, and European geographies (apt to err, of course, in matters of detail) usually locate it in America.

Having regard to the healthy mutual jealousy of the great towns, I feel that I am carrying audacity to the point of foolhardiness when I state that the streets of every American city I saw reminded me on the whole rather strongly of the streets of all the others. What inhabitants of what city could forgive this? Yet I must state it. Much of what I have said of the streets of New York applies, in my superficial opinion, for instance, to the streets of Chicago. It is well known that to the Chinaman all Westerners look alike. No tourist on his first visit to a country so astonishing as the United States is very different from a Chinaman; the tourist should reconcile himself to that deep truth. It is desolating to think that a second visit will reveal to me the blindness, the distortions, and the wrong-headedness of my first. But even as a Chinaman I did notice subtle differences between New York and Chicago. As one who was brought up in a bleak and uncanny climate, where soft coal is in universal use, I at once felt more at home in Chicago than I could ever do in New York. The old instinct to wash the hands and change the collar every couple of hours instantly returned to me in Chicago, together with the old comforting conviction that a harsh climate is a climate healthy for body and spirit. And, because it is laden with soot, the air of Chicago is a great mystifier and beautifier. Atmospheric effects may be seen there that are unobtainable without the combustion of soft coal. Talk, for example, as much as you please about the electric sky-signs of Broadway—not all of them together will write as much poetry on the sky as the single word "Illinois" that hangs without a clue to its suspension in the murky dusk over Michigan Avenue. The visionary aspects of Chicago are incomparable.

A WINTER MORNING IN LINCOLN PARK, CHICAGO

STREETS

Another difference, of quite another order, between New York and Chicago is that Chicago is self-conscious. New York is not; no metropolis ever is. You are aware of the self-consciousness of Chicago as soon as you are aware of its bitumen. The quality demands sympathy, and wins it by its wistfulness. Chicago is openly anxious about its soul. I liked that. I wish I could see a livelier anxiety concerning the municipal soul in certain cities of Europe.

Perhaps the least subtle difference between New York and Chicago springs from the fact that the handsomest part of New York is the center of New York, whereas the center of Chicago is disappointing. It does not impress. I was shown, in the center of Chicago, the first sky-scraper that the world had ever seen. I visited with admiration what was said to be the largest department store in the world. I visited with a natural rapture the largest book-store in the world. I was informed (but respectfully doubt) that Chicago is the greatest port in the world. I could easily credit, from the evidence of my own eyes, that it is the greatest railway center in the world. But still my imagination was not fired, as it has been fired again and again by far lesser and far less interesting places. Nobody could call Wabash Avenue spectacular, and nobody surely would assert that State Street is on a plane with the collective achievements of the city of which it is the principal thoroughfare. The truth is that Chicago lacks at present a rallying-point—some Place de la Concorde or Arc de Triomphe—something for its biggest streets to try to live up to. A convocation of elevated railroads is not enough. It seemed to me that Jackson Boulevard or Van Buren Street, with fine crescents abutting opposite Grant Park and Garfield Park, and a magnificent square at the intersection of Ashland Avenue, might ultimately be the chief sight and exemplar of Chicago. Why not? Should not the leading thoroughfare lead boldly' to the lake instead of shunning it? I anticipate the time when the municipal soul of Chicago will have found in its streets as adequate expression as it has already found in its boulevards.

Perhaps if I had not made the "grand tour" of those boulevards, I might have been better satisfied with the streets of Chicago. The excursion, in an automobile, occupied something like half of a frosty day that ended in torrents of rain—apparently a typical autumn day in Chicago! Before it had proceeded very far I knew that there was a sufficient creative imagination on the shore of Lake Michigan to carry through any municipal enterprise, however vast, to a generous and final conclusion. The conception of those boulevards discloses a tremendous audacity and faith. And as you roll along the macadam, threading at intervals a wide-stretching park, you are overwhelmed—at least I was—by the completeness of the scheme's execution and the lavishness with which the system is in every detail maintained and kept up.

You stop to inspect a conservatory, and find yourself in a really marvelous landscape garden, set with statues, all under glass and heated, where the gaffers of Chicago are collected together to discuss interminably the exciting politics of a city anxious about its soul. And while

A RIVER-FRONT HARMONY IN BLACK AND WHITE—CHICAGO

listening to them with one ear, with the other you may catch the laconic tale of a park official's perilous and successful vendetta against the forces of graft.

And then you resume the circuit and accomplish many more smooth, curving, tree-lined miles, varied by a jolting section, or by the faint odor of the Stock-yards, or by a halt to allow the longest freight-train in the world to cross your path. You have sighted in the distance universities, institutions, even factories; you have passed through many inhabited portions of the endless boulevard, but you have not actually touched hands with the city since you left it at the beginning of the ride. Then at last, as darkness falls, you feel that you are coming to the city again, but from another point of the compass. You have rounded the circle of its millions. You need only think of the unkempt, shabby, and tangled outskirts of New York, or of any other capital city, to realize the miracle that Chicago has put among her assets. . . .

You descry lanes of water in the twilight, and learn that in order to prevent her drainage from going into the lake Chicago turned a river back in its course and compelled it to discharge ultimately into the Mississippi. That is the story. You feel that it is exactly what Chicago, alone among cities, would have the imagination and the courage to do. Some man must have risen from his bed one morning with the idea, "Why not make the water flow the other way?" And then gone, perhaps diffidently, to his fellows in charge of the city with the suggestive query, "Why not make the water flow the other way?" And been laughed at! Only the thing was done in the end! I seem to have heard that there was an epilogue to this story, relating how certain other great cities showed a narrow objection to Chicago draining herself in the direction of the Mississippi, and how Chicago, after all, succeeded in persuading those whom it was necessary to persuade that, whereas her drainage was unsuited to Lake Michigan, it would consort well with the current of the Mississippi.

And then, in the night and in the rain, you swerve round some corner into the straight, by Grant Park, in full sight of one of the most dazzling spectacles that Chicago or any other city can offer—Michigan Avenue on a wet evening. Each of the thousands of electric standards in Michigan Avenue is a cluster of six huge globes (and yet they will tell you in Paris that the Rue de la Paix is the best-lit street in the world), and here and there is a red globe of warning. The two lines of light pour down their flame into the pool which is the roadway, and you travel continually toward an incandescent floor without ever quite reaching it, beneath mysterious words of fire hanging in the invisible sky! . . . The automobile stops. You get out, stiff, and murmur something inadequate about the length and splendor of those boulevards. "Oh," you are told, carelessly, "those are only the interior boulevards. . . . Nothing! You should see our exterior boulevards—not quite finished yet!"

III

THE CAPITOL AND OTHER SITES

III

THE CAPITOL AND OTHER SITES

"HERE, Jimmy!" said, briskly, a middle-aged administrative person in easy attire, who apparently had dominion over the whole floor beneath the dome. A younger man, also in easy attire, answered the call with an alert smile. The elder pointed sideways with his head at my two friends and myself, and commanded, "Run them through in thirty minutes!" Then, having reached the center of a cuspidor with all the precision of a character in a Californian novel, he added benevolently to Jimmy, "Make it a dollar for them." And Jimmy, consenting, led us away.

In this episode Europe was having her revenge on the United States, and I had planned it. How often, in half a hundred cities of Europe, had I not observed the American citizen seeing the sights thereof at high speed? Yes, even in front of the Michael Angelo sculptures in the Medici Chapel at Florence had I seen him, watch in hand, and heard him murmur "Bully!" to the sculptures and the time of the train to his wife in one breath! Now it was impossible for me to see Washington under the normal conditions of a session. And so I took advantage of the visit to Washington of two friends on business to see Washington hastily, as an excursionist pure and simple. I said to the United

States, grimly: "The most important and the most imposing thing in all America is surely the Capitol at Washington. Well, I will see it as you see the sacred sights of Europe. By me Europe shall be revenged."

' Thus it came about that we had hired a kind of carriage known as a "sea-going hack," driven by a negro in dark blue, who was even more picturesque than the negroes in white who did the menial work in the classic hotel, and had set forth frankly as excursionists into the streets of Washington, and presently through the celebrated Pennsylvania Avenue had achieved entrance into the Capitol.

It was a breathless pilgrimage—this seeing of the Capitol. And yet an impressive one. The Capitol is a great place. I was astonished—and I admit at once I ought not to have been astonished—that the Capitol appeals to the historic sense just as much as any other vast legislative palace of the world—and perhaps more intimately than some. The sequence of its endless corridors and innumerable chambers, each associated with event or tradition, begets awe. I think it was in the rich Senatorial reception-room that I first caught myself being surprised that the heavy gilded and marmoreal sumptuosity of the decorations recalled the average European palace. Why should I have been expecting the interior of the Capitol to consist of austere bare walls and unornamented floors? Perhaps it was due to some thought of Abraham Lincoln. But whatever its cause, the expectation was naïve and derogatory. The young guide, Jimmy, who by birth and genius evidently belonged to the universal race of guides, was

THE APPROACH TO THE CAPITOL

there to keep my ideas right and my eyes open. He was infinitely precious, and after his own fashion would have done honor to any public monument in the East. Such men are only bred in the very shadow of genuine history.

"See," he said, touching a wall. "Painted by celebrated Italian artist to look like bas-relief! But put your hand flat against it, and you'll see it isn't carved!" One might have been in Italy.

And a little later he was saying of other painting:

"Although painted in eighteen hundred sixty-five—forty-six years ago—you notice the flesh tints are as fresh as if painted yesterday!"

This, I think, was the finest remark I ever heard a guide make—until this same guide stepped in front of a portrait of Henry Clay, and, after a second's hesitation, threw off airily, patronizingly:

"Henry Clay—quite a good statesman!"

But I also contributed my excursionist's share to these singular conversations. In the swathed Senate Chamber I noticed two holland-covered objects that somehow reminded me of my youth and of religious dissent. I guessed that the daily proceedings of the Senate must be opened with devotional exercises, and these two objects seemed to me to be proper—why, I cannot tell—to the United States Senate; but there was one point that puzzled me.

"Why," I asked, "do you have *two* harmoniums?"

"Harmoniums, sir!" protested the guide, staggered. "Those are roll-top desks."

If only the floor could have opened and swallowed me

up, as it opens and swallows up the grand piano at the Thomas concerts in Chicago!

Neither the Senate Chamber nor the Congress Chamber was as imposing to me as the much less spacious former Senate Chamber and the former Congress Chamber. The old Senate Chamber, being now transferred to the uses of supreme justice, was closed on the day of our visit, owing to the funeral of a judge. Europeans would have acquiesced in the firm negative of its locked doors. But my friends, being American, would not acquiesce. The mere fact that the room was not on view actually sharpened their desire that I should see it. They were deaf to refusals. . . . I saw that room. And I was glad that I saw it, for in its august simplicity it was worth seeing. The spirit of the early history of the United States seemed to reside in that hemicycle; and the crape on the vacated and peculiar chair added its own effect.

My first notion on entering the former Congress Chamber was that I was in presence of the weirdest collection of ugly statues that I had ever beheld. Which impression, the result of shock, was undoubtedly false. On reflection I am convinced that those statues of the worthies of the different States are not more ugly than many statues I could point to in no matter what fane, museum, or palace of Europe. Their ugliness is only different from our accustomed European ugliness. The most crudely ugly mural decorations in the world are to be found all over Italy—the home of sublime frescos. The most atrociously debased architecture in the world is to be found in France—the home of sober artistic

52

ON PENNSYLVANIA AVENUE

tradition. Europe is simply peppered everywhere with sculpture whose appalling mediocrity defies competition. But when the European meets ugly sculpture or any ugly form of art in the New World, his instinct is to exclaim, "Of course!" His instinct is to exclaim, "This beats everything!" The attitude will not bear examination. And lo! I was adopting it myself.

"And here's Frances Willard!" cried, ecstatically, a young woman in one of the numerous parties of excursionists whose more deliberate paths through the Capitol we were continually crossing in our swift course.

And while, upon the spot where John Quincy Adams fell, I pretended to listen to the guide, who was proving to me from a distance that the place was as good a whispering-gallery as any in Europe, I thought: "And why should not Frances Willard's statue be there? I am glad it is there. And I am glad to see these groups of provincials admiring with open mouths the statues of the makers of their history, though the statues are chiefly painful." And I thought also: "New York may talk, and Chicago may talk, and Boston may talk, but it is these groups of provincials who are the real America." They were extraordinarily like people from the Five Towns—that is to say, extraordinarily like comfortable average people everywhere.

We were outside again, under one of the enormous porticos of the Capitol. The guide was receiving his well-earned dollar. The faithful fellow had kept nicely within the allotted limit of half an hour.

"Now we'll go and see the Congressional Library," said my particular friend.

But I would not. I had put myself in a position to retort to any sight-seeing American in Europe that I had seen his Capitol in thirty minutes, and I was content. I determined to rest on my laurels. Moreover, I had discovered that conventional sight-seeing is a very exhausting form of activity. I would visit neither the Library of Congress, nor the Navy Department, nor the Pension Bureau, nor the Dead-Letter Museum, nor the Zoological Park, nor the White House, nor the National Museum, nor the Lincoln Museum, nor the Smithsonian Institution, nor the Treasury, nor any other of the great spectacles of Washington. We just resumed the sea-going hack and drove indolently to and fro in avenues and parks, tasting the general savor of the city's large pleasantness. And we had not gone far before we got into the clutches of the police.

"I don't know who you are," said a policeman, as he stopped our sea-going hack. "I don't know who you are," he repeated, cautiously, as one accustomed to policing the shahs and grand viziers of the earth, "but it's my duty to tell you your coachman crossed over on the wrong side of the lamp-post. It's not allowed, and he knows it as well as I do."

We admitted by our shamed silence that we had no special "pull" in Washington; the wise negro said not a word; and we crept away from the policeman's wrath, and before I knew it we were up against the Washington Monument—one of those national calamities which ultimately happen to every country, and of which the supreme example is, of course, the Albert Memorial in Kensington Gardens.

ON THE STEPS OF THE PORTICO—THE CAPITOL

THE CAPITOL AND OTHER SITES

When I drove into the magnificent railway station late that night—true American rain was descending in sheets —I was carrying away with me an impression, as it were, of a gigantic plantation of public edifices in a loose tangle and undergrowth of thoroughfares: which seemed proper for a legislative and administrative metropolis. I was amused to reflect how the city, like most cities, had extended in precisely the direction in which its founders had never imagined it would extend; and naturally I was astonished by the rapidity of its development. (One of my friends, who was not old, had potted wild game in a marsh that is now a park close to the Capitol.) I thought that the noble wings of the Capitol were architecturally much superior to the central portion of it. I remembered a dazzling glimpse of the White House as a distinguished little building. I feared that ere my next visit the indefatigable energy of America would have rebuilt Pennsylvania Avenue, especially the higgledy-piggledy and picturesque and untidy portion of it that lies nearest to the Capitol, and I hoped that in doing so the architects would at any rate not carry the cornice to such excess as it has been carried in other parts of the town. And, finally, I was slightly scared by the prevalence of negroes. It seemed to me as if in Washington I had touched the fringe of the negro problem.

✽

It was in a different and a humbler spirit that I went to Boston. I had received more warnings and more advice about Boston than about all the other cities put together. And, in particular, the greatest care had been

taken to permeate my whole being with the idea that
Boston was "different." In some ways it proved so to
be. One difference forced itself upon me immediately
I left the station for the streets—the quaint, original
odor of the taxis. When I got to the entirely admirable
hotel I found a book in a prominent situation on the
writing-table in my room. In many hotels this book
would have been the Bible. But here it was the catalogue of the hotel library; it ran to a hundred and eighty-
two pages. On the other hand, there was no bar in the
hotel, and no smoking-room. I make no comments; I
draw no conclusions; I state the facts.

The warnings continued after my arrival. I was informed by I don't know how many persons that Boston
was "a circular city," with a topography calculated to
puzzle the simple. This was true. I usually go about
in strange places with a map, but I found the map of
Boston even more complex than the city it sought to
explain. If I did not lose myself, it was because I never
trusted myself alone; other people lost me.

Within an hour or so I had been familiarized by
Bostonians with a whole series of apparently stock
jokes concerning and against Boston, such as that one
hinging on the phrase "cold roast Boston," and that
other one about the best thing in Boston being the five
o'clock train to New York (I do not vouch for the hour
of departure). Even in Cambridge, a less jocular place,
a joke seemed to be immanent, to the effect that though
you could always tell a Harvard man, you could not tell
him much.

Matters more serious awaited me. An old resident

56

UNDER THE GREAT DOME OF THE CAPITOL

of Boston took me out for privacy onto the Common and whispered in my ear: "This is the most snobbish city in the whole world. There is no real democracy here. The first thing people do when they get to know you is to show you their family tree and prove that they came over in the *Mayflower*." And so he ran on, cursing Boston up hill and down dale. Nevertheless, he was very proud of his Boston. Had I agreed with the condemnation, he might have thrown me into the artificial brook. Another great Bostonian expert, after leading me on to admit that I had come in order to try to learn the real Boston, turned upon me with ferocious gaiety, thus: "You will not learn the real Boston. You cannot. The real Boston is the old Back Bay folk, who gravitate eternally between Beacon Street and State Street and the Somerset Club, and never go beyond. They confuse New England with the created universe, and it is impossible that you should learn them. Nobody could learn them in less than twenty years' intense study and research."

Cautioned, and even intimidated, I thought it would be safest just to take Boston as Boston came, respectfully but casually. And as the hospitality of Boston was prodigious, splendid, unintermittent, and most delightfully unaffected, I had no difficulty whatever in taking Boston as she came. And my impressions began to emerge, one after another, from the rich and cloudy confusion of novel sensations.

What primarily differentiates Boston from all the other cities I saw is this: It is finished; I mean complete. Of the other cities, while admitting their actual achieve-

ment, one would say, and their own citizens invariably
do say, "They will be . . ." Boston is.

Another leading impression, which remains with me,
is that Boston is not so English as it perhaps imagines
itself to be. An interviewer (among many) came to
see me about Boston, and he came with the fixed and sole
notion in his head that Boston was English. He would
have it that Boston was English. Worn down by his
persistency, I did, as a fact, admit in one obscure corner of the interview that Boston had certain English
characteristics. The scare-head editor of the interviewing paper, looking through his man's copy for suitable
prey, came across my admission. It was just what he
wanted; it was what he was thirsting for. In an instant
the scare-head was created: "Boston as English as a
muffin!" An ideal scare-head! That I had never used
the word "muffin" or any such phrase was a detail ex-
quisitely unimportant. The scare-head was immense.
It traveled in fine large type across the continent. I met
it for weeks afterward in my press-cuttings, and I doubt
if Boston was altogether delighted with the comparison.
I will not deny that Boston is less strikingly un-English
than sundry other cities. I will not deny that I met men
in Boston of a somewhat pronounced English type. I
will not deny that in certain respects old Kensington
reminds me of a street here and there in Boston—such
as Mount Vernon Street or Chestnut Street. But I do
maintain that the Englishness of Boston has been seriously exaggerated.

And still another very striking memory of Boston—
indeed, perhaps, the paramount impression!—is that it

contains the loveliest modern thing I saw in America—
namely, the Puvis de Chavannes wall-paintings on the
grand staircase of the Public Library. The Library itself
is a beautiful building, but it holds something more
beautiful. Never shall I forget my agitation on beholding these unsurpassed works of art, which alone would
suffice to make Boston a place of pilgrimage.

When afterward I went back to Paris, the painters'
first question was: *"Et les Puvis à Boston—vous les avez
vus? Qu'est-ce que vous en dites?"*

It was very un-English on the part of Boston to com-
mission these austere and classical works. England
would never have done it. The nationality of the
greatest decorative painter of modern times would have
offended her sense of fitness. What—a French painter
officially employed on an English public building?
Unthinkable! England would have insisted on an English painter—or, at worst, an American. It is strange
that a community which had the wit to honor itself
by employing Puvis de Chavannes should be equally
enthusiastic about the frigid theatricalities of an E. A.
Abbey or the forbidding and opaque intricate dexterity
of a John Sargent in the same building. Or, rather, it is
not strange, for these contradictions are discoverable
everywhere in the patronage of the arts.

It was from the Public Library that some friends and
I set out on a little tour of Boston. Whether we went
north, south, east, or west I cannot tell, for this was one
of the few occasions when the extreme variousness of a
city has deprived me definitely of a sense of direction;
but I know that we drove many miles through magnifi-

cent fenny parks, whose roads were reserved to pleasure, and that at length, after glimpsing famous houses and much of the less centralized wealth and ease of Boston, we came out upon the shores of the old harbor, and went into a yacht-club-house with a glorious prospect. Boston has more book-shops to the acre than any city within my knowledge except Aberdeen (not North Carolina, but Scotland). Its book-shops, however, are as naught to its yacht clubs. And for one yacht club I personally would sacrifice many book-shops. It was an exciting moment in my life when, after further wandering on and off coast roads, and through curving, cobbled, rackety streets, and between thunderous tram-cars and under deafening elevated lines, I was permitted to enter the celestial and calm precincts of the Boston Yacht Club itself, which overlooks another harbor. The acute and splendid nauticality of this club, all fashioned out of an old warehouse, stamps Boston as a city which has comprehended the sea. I saw there the very wheel of the *Spray*, the cockboat in which the regretted Slocum wafted himself round the world! I sat in an arm-chair which would have suited Falstaff, and whose tabular arms would have held all Falstaff's tankards, and gazed through a magnified port-hole at a six-masted schooner as it crossed the field of vision! And I had never even dreamed that a six-masted schooner existed! It was with difficulty that I left the Boston Yacht Club. Indeed, I would only leave it in order to go and see the frigate *Constitution*, the ship which was never defeated, and which assuredly, after over a hundred and ten years of buoyant life, remains the most truly English thing

THE PROMENADE—CITY POINT, BOSTON

City Point

in Boston. The afternoon teas of Boston are far less English than that grim and majestic craft.

We passed into the romantic part of Boston, skirting vast wool-warehouses and other enormous establishments bearing such Oriental signs as "Coffee and Spices." And so into a bewildering congeries of crowded streets, where every name on the walls seemed to be Italian, and where every corner was dangerous with vegetable-barrows, tram-cars, and perambulators; through this quarter the legend of Paul Revere seemed to float like a long wisp of vapor. And then I saw the Christopher Wren spire of Paul Revere's signal-church, closed now— but whether because the congregation had dwindled to six or for some more recondite reason I am not clear. And then I beheld the delightful, elegant fabric of the old State House, with the memories of massacre round about it, and the singular spectacle of the Lion and the Unicorn on its roof. Too proudly negligent had Boston been to remove those symbols!

And finally we rolled into the central and most circular shopping quarter, as different from the Italian quarter as the Italian quarter was different from Copley Square; and its heart was occupied by a graveyard. And here I had to rest.

The second portion of the itinerary began with the domed State Capitol, an impressive sight, despite its strange coloring, and despite its curious habit of illuminating itself at dark, as if in competition with such establishments as the "Bijou Dream," on the opposite side of the Common. Here I first set eyes on Beacon Street, familiar—indeed, classic—to the European student of American literature. Commonwealth Avenue, I have to confess, I had never heard of till I saw it. These interminable and gorgeous thoroughfares, where each massive abode is a costly and ceremonial organization of the most polished and civilized existence, leave the simple European speechless—especially when he remembers the swampy origin of the main part of the ground. . . . The inscrutable, the unknowable Back Bay!

Here, indeed, is evidence of a society in equilibrium, and therefore of a society which will receive genuinely new ideas with an extreme, if polite, caution, while welcoming with warm suavity old ideas that disguise themselves as novelties!

It was a tremendous feat to reclaim from ooze the foundation of Back Bay. Such feats are not accomplished in Europe; they are not even imaginatively conceived there. And now that the great business is achieved, the energy that did it, restless and unoccupied, is seeking another field. I was informed that Boston is dreaming of the construction of an artificial island in the midst of the river Charles, with the hugest cathedral in the world thereon, and the most gorgeous bridges that ever spanned a fine stream. With proper deference, it is to be hoped that Boston, forgetting this infelicitous caprice, will remember in time that she alone among the great cities of America is complete. A project that would consort well with the genius of Chicago might disserve Boston in the eyes of those who esteem a sense of fitness to be among the major qualifications for the true art of life. And, in the matter of the art of daily living, Boston as she is has a great deal to teach to the rest of the country, and little to learn. Such is the diffident view of a stranger.

❦

Cambridge is separated from Boston by the river Charles and by piquant jealousies that tickle no one more humorously than those whom, theoretically, they stab. From the east bank Cambridge is academic, and there-fore negligible; from the west, Boston dwindles to a mere quay where one embarks for Europe.

What struck me first about Cambridge was that it must be the only city of its size and amenity in the United States without an imposing hotel. It is difficult to imagine any city in the United States minus at least two imposing hotels, with a barber's shop in the basement and a world's fair in the hall. But one soon perceives that Cambridge is a city apart. In visual characteristics it must have changed very little, and it will never change with facility. Boston is pre-eminently a town of tradi-tions, but the traditions have to be looked for. Cam-bridge is equally a town of traditions, but the traditions stare you in the face.

My first halt was in front of the conspicuous home of James Russell Lowell. Now in the far recesses of the Five Towns I was brought up on "My Study Windows." My father, who would never accept the authority of an encyclopedia when his children got him in a corner on some debated question of fact, held James Russell Lowell as the supreme judge of letters, from whom not even he could appeal. (It is true, he had never heard of Ste. Beuve, and regarded Matthew Arnold as a modern fad.) And there were the study windows of James

Russell Lowell! And his house in its garden was only one of hundreds of similar houses standing in like old gardens.

It was highly agreeable to learn that some of the pre-Revolution houses had not yet left the occupation of the families which built them. Beautiful houses, a few of them, utterly dissimilar from anything on the other side of the Atlantic! Did not William Morris always maintain that wood was and forever would be the most suitable material for building a house? On the side of the railroad track near Toledo I saw frame houses, whose architecture is debased from this Cambridge architecture, blown clean over by the gale. But the gale that will deracinate Cambridge has not yet begun to rage. . . . I rejoiced to see the house of Longfellow. In spite of the fact that he wrote "The Wreck of the *Hesperus*," he seems to keep his position as the chief minor poet of the English language. And the most American and the most wistful thing in Cambridge was that the children of Cambridge had been guided to buy and make inalienable the land in front of his house, so that his descendant might securely enjoy the free prospect that Longfellow enjoyed. In what other country would just such a delicate, sentimental homage have been paid in just such an ingeniously fanciful manner?[1]

---

[1] This story was related to me by a resident of Cambridge. Mr. Richard H. Dana, Longfellow's son-in-law, has since informed me that it is quite untrue. I regret that it is quite untrue. It ought to have been quite true. The land in question was given by Longfellow's children to the Longfellow Memorial Association, who gave it to the city of Cambridge. The general children of Cambridge did give to Longfellow an arm-chair made from the wood of a certain historic "spreading chestnut-tree," under which stood a certain historic village smithy; and with this I suppose I must be content.—A. B.

THE BOSTON YACHT CLUB—OVERLOOKING THE HARBOR

THE CAPITOL AND OTHER SITES

After I had passed the Longfellow house it began to rain, and dusk began to gather in the recesses between the houses; and my memory is that, with an athletic and tireless companion, I walked uncounted leagues through endless avenues of Cambridge homes toward a promised club that seemed ever to retreat before us with the shyness of a fawn. However, we did at length capture it. This club was connected with Harvard, and I do not propose to speak of Harvard in the present chapter.

The typical Cambridge house as I saw it persists in my recollection as being among the most characteristic and comfortable of "real" American phenomena. And one reason why I insisted, in a previous chapter, on the special Americanism of Indianapolis is that Indianapolis is full of a modified variety of these houses which is even more characteristically American—to my mind—than the Cambridge style itself. Indianapolis being by general consent the present chief center of letters in the United States, it is not surprising that I, an author, knew more people from Indianapolis than from any other city. Indeed, I went to Indianapolis simply because I had old friends there, and not at all in the hope of inspecting a city characteristically American. It was quite startlingly different from the mental picture I had formed of it.

I think that in order to savor Indianapolis properly one should approach it as I approached it—in an accommodation-train on a single track, a train with a happy-go-lucky but still agreeable service in its restaurant-car, a train that halts at every barn-door in the vast flat, featureless fields of yellow stubble, rolling sometimes over a muddy, brown river, and skirting now and then a welcome wooded cleft in the monotony of the landscape. The scenes at those barn-doors were full of the picturesque and of the racy. A farmer with a gun and a brace of rabbits and a dog leaping up at them, while two young women talked to or at the farmer from a distance; a fat little German girl in a Scotch frock, cleaning outside windows with the absorbed seriousness of a grandmother; a group of boys dividing their attention between her and the train; an old woman driving a cart, and a negro gesticulating and running after the cart; and all of them, save the nigger, wearing gloves—presumably as a protection against the strong wind that swept through the stubble and shook the houses and the few trees. Those houses, in all their summariness and primitive crudity, yet reminded one of the Cambridge homes; they exhibited some remains of the pre-Revolution style.

And then you come to the inevitable State Fair grounds, and the environs of the city which is the capital and heart of all those plains.

And after you have got away from the railroad station and the imposing hotels and the public monuments and the high central buildings—an affair of five minutes in an automobile—you discover yourself in long, calm streets of essential America. These streets are rectangular; the streets of Cambridge abhor the straight line. They are full everywhere of maple-trees. And on either side they are bordered with homes—each house detached, each house in its own fairly spacious garden, each house individual and different from all the rest. Few of the houses are large; on the other hand, none of them is small: this is the region of the solid middle class, the class which loves comfort and piques itself on its amenities, but is a little ashamed or too timid to be luxurious.

Architecturally the houses represent a declension from the purity of earlier Cambridge. Scarcely one is really beautiful. The style is debased. But then, it possesses the advantage of being modernized; it has not the air of having strayed by accident into the wrong century. And, moreover, it is saved from condemnation by its sobriety and by its honest workmanship. It is the expression of a race incapable of looking foolish, of being giddy, of running to extremes. It is the expression of a race that both clung to the past and reached out to the future; that knew how to make the best of both worlds; that keenly realized the value of security because it had been through insecurity. You can see that all these houses were built by people who loved "a bit of property," and to whom a safe and dignified roof was the final ambition achieved. Why! I do believe that there are men and women behind some of those curtains to this day who haven't quite realized that the Indians aren't coming any more, and that there is permanently enough wood in the pile, and that quinine need no longer figure in the store cupboard as a staple article of diet! I do believe that there are minor millionaires in some of those drawing-rooms who wonder whether, out-soaring the ambition of a bit of property, they would be justified

in creeping down-town and buying a cheap automobile!
... These are the people who make the link between
the academic traditionalism of Cambridge and such excessively modern products of evolution as their own
mayor, Mr. Shanks, protector of the poor. They are
not above forming deputations to parley with their own
mayor. . . . I loved them. Their drawing-rooms were
full of old silver, and book-gossip, and Victorian ladies
apparently transported direct from the more aristocratic
parts of the Five Towns, who sat behind trays and
poured out tea from the identical tea-pot that my grandmother used to keep in a green bag.

In the outer suburbs of the very largest cities I saw
revulsions against the wholesale barracky conveniences
of the apartment-house, in the shape of little colonies
of homes, consciously but superficially imitating the
Cambridge-Indianapolis tradition—with streets far more
curvily winding than the streets of Cambridge, and
sidewalks of a strip of concrete between green turf-
bands that recalled the original sidewalks of Indianapolis and even of the rural communities around Indianapolis. Cozy homes, each in its own garden, with
its own clothes-drier, and each different from all the
rest! Homes that the speculative builder, recking not
of the artistic sobriety, had determined should be picturesque at any cost of capricious ingenuity! And not
secure homes, because, though they were occupied by
their owners, their owners had not built them—had only
bought them, and would sell them as casually as they
had bought. The apartment-house will probably prove
stronger than these throwbacks. And yet the time

will come when even the apartment-house will be regarded as a picturesque survival. Into what novel architecture and organization of living it will survive I should not care to prophesy, but I am convinced that the future will be quite as interestingly human as the present is, and as the past was.

IV

SOME ORGANIZATIONS

IV

SOME ORGANIZATIONS

WHAT strikes and frightens the backward European
as much as anything in the United States is the
efficiency and fearful universality of the telephone.
Just as I think of the big cities as agglomerations pierced
everywhere by elevator-shafts full of movement, so I
think of them as being threaded, under pavements and
over roofs and between floors and ceilings and between
walls, by millions upon millions of live filaments that
unite all the privacies of the organism—and destroy
them in order to make one immense publicity! I do
not mean that Europe has failed to adopt the telephone,
nor that in Europe there are no hotels with the dreadful
curse of an active telephone in every room. But I do
mean that the European telephone is a toy, and a somewhat clumsy one, compared with the inexorable seriousness of the American telephone. Many otherwise highly
civilized Europeans are as timid in addressing a telephone as they would be in addressing a royal sovereign.
The average European middle-class householder still
speaks of his telephone, if he has one, in the same
falsely casual tone as the corresponding American is
liable to speak of his motor-car. It is naught—a negligible trifle—but somehow it comes into the conversation!
"How odd!" you exclaim. And you are right. It is

73

we Europeans who are wrong, through no particular fault of our own.

The American is ruthlessly logical about the tele-phone. The only occasion on which I was in really serious danger of being taken for a madman in the United States was when, in a Chicago hotel, I permanent-ly removed the receiver from the telephone in a room designed (doubtless ironically) for slumber. The whole hotel was appalled. Half Chicago shuddered. In re-sponse to the prayer of a deputation from the manage-ment I restored the receiver. On the horrified face of the deputation I could read the unspoken query: "Is it conceivable that you have been in this country a month without understanding that the United States is primarily nothing but a vast congeries of telephone-cabins?" Yes, I yielded and admired! And I surmise that on my next visit I shall find a telephone on every table of every restaurant that respects itself.

It is the efficiency of the telephone that makes it irresistible to a great people whose passion is to "get results"—the instancy with which the communication is given, and the clear loudness of the telephone's voice in reply to yours: phenomena utterly unknown in Europe. Were I to inhabit the United States, I too should become a victim of the telephone habit, as it is practised in its most advanced form in those suburban communities to which I have already incidentally referred at the end of the previous chapter. There a woman takes to the telephone as women in more decadent lands take to morphia. You can see her at morn at her bedroom window, pouring confidences into her telephone, thus

74

AT MORN POURING CONFIDENCES INTO HER TELEPHONE

combining the joy of an innocent vice with the healthy freshness of breeze and sunshine. It has happened to me to sit in a drawing-room, where people gathered round the telephone as Europeans gather round a fire, and to hear immediately after the ejaculation of a number into the telephone a sharp ring from outside through the open window, and then to hear in answer to the question, "What are you going to wear to-night?" two absolutely simultaneous replies, one loudly from the telephone across the room, and the other faintlier from a charming human voice across the garden: "I don't know. What are you?" Such may be the pleasing secondary scientific effect of telephoning to the lady next door on a warm afternoon.

Now it was obvious that behind the apparently simple exterior aspects of any telephone system there must be an intricate and marvelous secret organization. In Europe my curiosity would probably never have been excited by the thought of that organization—at home one accepts everything as of course!—but, in the United States, partly because the telephone is so much more wonderful and terrible there, and partly because in a foreign land one is apt to have strange caprices, I allowed myself to become the prey of a desire to see the arcanum concealed at the other end of all the wires; and thus, one day, under the high protection of a demigod of the electrical world, I paid a visit to a telephone-exchange in New York, and saw therein what nine hundred and ninety-nine out of every thousand of the most ardent telephone-users seldom think about and will never see.

A murmuring sound, as of an infinity of scholars in a

prim school conning their lessons, and a long row of
young women seated in a dim radiance on a long row of
precisely similar stools, before a long apparatus of holes
and pegs and pieces of elastic cord, all extremely intent:
that was the first broad impression. One saw at once
that none of these young women had a single moment
to spare; they were all involved in the tremendous
machine, part of it, keeping pace with it and in it, and
not daring to take their eyes off it for an instant, lest
they should sin against it. What they were droning
about it was impossible to guess; for if one stationed oneself close to any particular rapt young woman, she seemed
to utter no sound, but simply and without ceasing to peg
and unpeg holes at random among the thousands of
holes before her, apparently in obedience to the signaling
of faint, tiny lights that in thousands continually ex-
pired and were rekindled. (It was so that these tiny
lights should be distinguishable that the illumination
of the secret and finely appointed chamber was kept
dim.) Throughout the whole length of the apparatus
the colored elastic cords to which the pegs were attached
kept crossing one another in fantastic patterns.

We who had entered were ignored. We might have
been ghosts, invisible and inaudible. Even the supervisors, less-young women set in authority, did not turn
to glance at us as they moved restlessly peering behind
the stools. And yet somehow I could hear the delicate
shoulders of all the young women saying, without
speech: "Here come these tyrants and taskmasters
again, who have invented this exercise which nearly but
not quite cracks our little brains for us! They know

exactly how much they can get out of us, and they get it. They are cleverer than us and more powerful than us; and we have to submit to their discipline. But—" And afar off I could hear: "What are you going to wear to-night?" "Will you dine with me to-night?" "I want two seats." "Very well, thanks, and how is Mrs. . . . ?" "When can I see you to-morrow?" "I'll take your offer for those bonds." . . . And I could see the interiors of innumerable offices and drawing-rooms. . . . But of course I could hear and see nothing really except the intent drone and quick gesturing of those completely absorbed young creatures in the dim radiance, on stools precisely similar.

I understood why the telephone service was so efficient. I understood not merely from the demeanor of the long row of young women, but from everything else I had seen in the exact and diabolically ingenious ordering of the whole establishment.

We were silent for a time, as though we had entered a church. We were, perhaps unconsciously, abashed by the intensity of the absorption of these neat young women. After a while one of the guides, one of the inscrutable beings who had helped to invent and construct the astounding organism, began in a low voice on the forlorn hope of making me comprehend the mechanism of a telephone-call and its response. And I began on the forlorn hope of persuading him by intelligent acting that I did comprehend. We each made a little progress. I could not tell him that, though I genuinely and humbly admired his particular variety of genius, what interested me in the affair was not the mechanics, but the human equation. As a professional reader of faces, I glanced as well as I could sideways at those bent girls' faces to see if they were happy. An absurd inquiry! Do *I* look happy when I'm at work, I wonder! Did they then look reasonably content? Well, I came to the conclusion that they looked like most other faces—neither one thing nor the other. Still, in a great establishment, I would sooner search for sociological information in the faces of the employed than in the managerial rules.

"What do they earn?" I asked, when we emerged from the ten-atmosphere pressure of that intense absorption. (Of course I knew that no young women could possibly for any length of time be as intensely absorbed as these appeared to be. But the illusion was there, and it was effective.)

I learned that even the lowest beginner earned five dollars a week. It was just the sum I was paying for a pair of clean sheets every night at a grand hotel. And that the salary rose to six, seven, eight, eleven, and even fourteen dollars for supervisors, who, however, had to stand on their feet seven and a half hours a day, as shop-girls do for ten hours a day; and that in general the girls had thirty minutes for lunch, and a day off every week, and that the Company supplied them gratuitously with tea, coffee, sugar, couches, newspapers, arm-chairs, and fresh air, of which last fifty fresh cubic feet were pumped in for every operator every minute.

"Naturally," I was told, "the discipline is strict. There are test wires. . . . We can check the 'time elements.' . . . We keep a record of every call. They'll take a dollar

a week less in an outside place—for instance, a hotel. . . .
Their average stay here is thirty months."

And I was told the number of exchanges there were in
New York, exactly like the one I was seeing.

A dollar a week less in a hotel! How feminine! And
how masculine! And how wise for one sort of young
woman, and how foolish for another! . . . Imagine
quitting that convent with its guaranteed fresh air,
and its couches and sugar and so on, for the rough
hazards and promiscuities of a hotel! On the other
hand, imagine not quitting it!

Said the demigod of the electrical world, condescend-
ingly: "All this telephone business is done on a mere few
hundred horse-power. Come away, and I'll show you
electricity in bulk."

And I went away with him, thoughtful. In spite
of the inhuman perfection of its functioning, that exchange was a very human place indeed. It brilliantly
solved some problems; it raised others. Excessively
difficult to find any fault whatever in it! A marvelous
service, achieved under strictly hygienic conditions—
and young women must make their way through the
world! And yet— Yes, a very human place indeed!

❈

The demigods of the electric world do not condescend
to move about in petrol motor-cars. In the exercise
of a natural and charming coquetry they insist on electrical traction, and it was in the most modern and sound-
less electric brougham that we arrived at nightfall
under the overhanging cornice-eaves of two gigantic
Florentine palaces—just such looming palaces, they

appeared in the dark, as may be seen in any central
street of Florence, with a cinema-show blazing its signs
on the ground floor, and Heaven knows what remnants
of Italian aristocracy in the mysterious upper stories.
Having entered one of the palaces, simultaneously with
a tornado of wind, we passed through long, deserted,
narrow galleries, lined with thousands of small, caged
compartments containing "transformers," and on each
compartment was a label bearing always the same words:
"Danger, 6,600 volts." "Danger, 6,600 volts." "Danger, 6,600 volts." A wondrous relief when we had
escaped with our lives from the menace of those innumerable volts! And then we stood on a high platform surrounded by handles, switches, signals—apparatus enough
to put all New York into darkness, or to annihilate it
in an instant by the unloosing of terrible cohorts of
volts!—and faced an enormous white hall, sparsely
peopled by a few colossal machines that seemed to be
revolving and oscillating about their business with the
fatalism of conquered and resigned leviathans. Im-
maculately clean, inconceivably tidy, shimmering with
brilliant light under its lofty and beautiful ceiling,
shaking and roaring with the terrific thunder of its own
vitality, this hall in which no common voice could make
itself heard produced nevertheless an effect of magical
stillness, silence, and solitude. We were alone in it,
save that now and then in the far-distant spaces a figure
might flit and disappear between the huge glinting
columns of metal. It was a hall enchanted and in-
explicable. I understood nothing of it. But I understood that half the electricity of New York was being

generated by its engines of a hundred and fifty thousand horse-power, and that if the spell were lifted the elevators of New York would be immediately paralyzed, and the twenty million lights expire beneath the eyes of a startled population. I could have gazed at it to this day, and brooded to this day upon the human imaginations that had perfected it; but I was led off, hypnotized, to see the furnaces and boilers under the earth. And even there we were almost alone, to such an extent had one sort of senseless matter been compelled to take charge of another sort of senseless matter. The odyssey of the coal that was lifted high out of ships on the tide beyond, to fall ultimately into the furnaces within, scarcely touched by the hand-wielded shovel, was by itself epical. Fresh air pouring in at the rate of twenty-four million cubic feet per hour cooled the entire palace, and gave to these stoke-holes the uncanny quality of refrigerators. The lowest horror of the steamship had been abolished here.

I was tempted to say: "This alone is fit to be called the heart of New York!"

They took me to the twin palace, and on the windy way thither figures were casually thrown at me. As that a short circuit may cause the machines to surge wildly into the sudden creation of six million horse-power of electricity, necessitating the invention of other machines to control automatically these perilous vagaries! As that in the down-town district the fire-engine was being abolished because, at a signal, these power-houses could in thirty seconds concentrate on any given main a pressure of three hundred pounds to the square inch, lifting jets of water perhaps above the roofs of sky-scrapers! As that the city could fine these power-houses at the rate of five hundred dollars a minute for any interruption of the current longer than three minutes—but the current had never failed for a single second! As that in one year over two million dollars' worth of machinery had been scrapped! ... And I was aware that it was New York I was in, and not Timbuctoo.

In the other palace it appeared that the great American scrapping process was even yet far from complete. At first sight this other seemed to resemble the former one, but I was soon instructed that the former one was as naught to this one, for here the turbine—the "strong, silent man" among engines—was replacing the racket of cylinder and crank. Statistics are tiresome and futile to stir the imagination. I disdain statistics, even when I assimilate them. And yet when my attention was directed to one trifling block of metal, and I was told that it was the most powerful "unit" in the world, and that it alone would make electricity sufficient for the lighting of a city of a quarter of a million people, I felt that statistics, after all, could knock you a stagger-ing blow. ... In this other palace, too, was the same solitude of machinery, attending most conscientiously and effectively to itself. A singularly disconcerting spectacle! And I reflected that, according to dreams already coming true, the telephone-exchange also would soon be a solitude of clicking contact-points, functioning in mystic certitude, instead of a convent of girls requiring sugar and couches, and thirsting for love. A singularly disconcerting prospect!

SOME ORGANIZATIONS

But was it necessary to come to America in order to see and describe telephone - exchanges and electrical power-houses? Do not these wonders exist in all the cities of earth? They do, but not to quite the same degree of wondrousness. Hat-shops, and fine hat-shops, exist in New York, but not to quite the same degree of wondrousness as in Paris. People sing in New York, but not with quite the same natural lyricism as in Naples. The great civilizations all present the same features; but it is just the differences in degree between the same feature in this civilization and in that—it is just these differences which together constitute and illustrate the idiosyncrasy of each. It seems to me that the brains and the imagination of America shone superlatively in the conception and ordering of its vast organizations of human beings, and of machinery, and of the two combined. By them I was more profoundly attracted, impressed, and inspired than by any other non-spiritual phenomena whatever in the United States. For me they were the proudest material achievements, and essentially the most poetical achievements, of the United States. And that is why I am dwelling on them.

❦

Further, there are business organizations in America of a species which do not flourish at all in Europe. For example, the "mail-order house," whose secrets were very generously displayed to me in Chicago—a peculiar establishment which sells merely everything (except patent-medicines)—on condition that you order it by post. Go into that house with money in your palm, and ask for a fan or a flail or a fur-coat or a fountain-

83

pen or a fiddle, and you will be requested to return home and write a letter about the proposed purchase, and stamp the letter and drop it into a mail-box, and then to wait till the article arrives at your door. That house is one of the most spectacular and pleasing proofs that the inhabitants of the United States are thinly scattered over an enormous area, in tiny groups, often quite isolated from stores. On the day of my visit sixty thousand letters had been received, and every executable order contained in these was executed before closing time, by the co-ordinated efforts of over four thousand female employees and over three thousand males. The conception would make Europe dizzy. Imagine a merchant in Moscow trying to inaugurate such a scheme!

A little machine no bigger than a soup-plate will open hundreds of envelops at once. They are all the same, those envelops; they have even less individuality than sheep being sheared, but when the contents of one—any one at random—are put into your hand, something human and distinctive is put into your hand. I read the caligraphy on a blue sheet of paper, and it was written by a woman in Wyoming, a neat, earnest, harassed, and possibly rather harassing woman, and she wanted all sorts of things and wanted them intensely—I could see that with clearness. This complex purchase was an important event in her year. So far as her imagination went, only one mail-order would reach the Chicago house that morning, and the entire establishment would be strained to meet it.

Then the blue sheet was taken from me and thrust into the system, and therein lost to me. I was taken to a mysteriously rumbling shaft of broad diameter, that pierced all the floors of the house and had trap-doors on each floor. And when one of the trap-doors was opened I saw packages of all descriptions racing after one another down spiral planes within the shaft. There were several of these great shafts—with divisions for mail, express, and freight traffic—and packages were ceaselessly racing down all of them, laden with the objects desired by the woman of Wyoming and her fifty-nine-thousand-odd fellow-customers of the day. At first it seemed to me impossible that that earnest, impatient woman in Wyoming should get precisely what she wanted; it seemed to me impossible that some mistake should not occur in all that noisy fever of rushing activity. But after I had followed an order, and seen it filled and checked, my opinion was that a mistake would be the most miraculous phenomenon in that establishment. I felt quite reassured on behalf of Wyoming.

And then I was suddenly in a room where six hundred billing-machines were being clicked at once by six hundred young women, a fantastic aural nightmare, though none of the young women appeared to be conscious that anything bizarre was going on. . . . And then I was in a printing-shop, where several lightning machines spent their whole time every day in printing the most popular work of reference in the United States, a bulky book full of pictures, with an annual circulation of five and a half million copies—the general catalogue of the firm. For the first time I realized the true meaning of the word "popularity"—and sighed. . . .

And then it was lunch-time for about a couple of thousand employees, and in the boundless restaurant I witnessed the working of the devices which enabled these legions to choose their meals, and pay for them (cost price) in a few moments, and without advanced mathematical calculations. The young head of the restaurant showed me, with pride, a menu of over a hundred dishes—Austrian, German, Hungarian, Italian, Scotch, French, and American; at prices from one cent up as high as ten cents (prime roast-beef)—and at the foot of the menu was his personal appeal: "*I* desire to extend to you a cordial invitation to inspect,". etc. "*My* constant aim will be," etc. Yet it was not *his* restaurant. It was the firm's restaurant. Here I had a curious illustration of an admirable characteristic of American business methods that was always striking me—namely, the real delegation of responsibility. An American board of direction will put a man in charge of a department, as a viceroy over a province, saying, as it were: "This is yours. Do as you please with it. We will watch the results." A marked contrast this with the centralizing of authority which seems to be ever proceeding in Europe, and which breeds in all classes at all ages—especially in France—a morbid fear and horror of accepting responsibility.

Later, I was on the ground level, in the midst of an enormous apparent confusion—the target for all the packages and baskets, big and little, that shot every instant in a continuous stream from those spiral planes, and slid dangerously at me along the floors. Here were the packers. I saw a packer deal with a collected

LUNCHEON IN A DOWN-TOWN CLUB

order, and in this order were a number of tiny cookery utensils, a four-cent curling-iron, a brush, and two incredibly ugly pink china mugs, inscribed in cheap gilt respectively with the words "Father" and "Mother." Throughout my stay in America no moment came to me more dramatically than this moment, and none has remained more vividly in my mind. All the daily domestic life of the small communities in the wilds of the West and the Middle West, and in the wilds of the back streets of the great towns, seemed to be revealed to me by the contents of that basket, as the packer wrapped up and protected one article after another. I had been compelled to abandon a visitation of the West and of the small communities everywhere, and I was sorry. But here in a microcosm I thought I saw the simple reality of the backbone of all America, a symbol of the millions of the little plain people, who ultimately make possible the glory of the world-renowned streets and institutions in dazzling cities.

There was something indescribably touching in that curling-iron and those two mugs. I could see the table on which the mugs would soon proudly stand, and "father" and "mother" and children thereat, and I could see the hand heating the curling-iron and applying it. I could see the whole little home and the whole life of the little home. . . . And afterward, as I wandered through the warehouses—pyramids of the same chair, cupboards full of the same cheap violin, stacks of the same album of music, acres of the same carpet and wall-paper, tons of the same gramophone, hundreds of tons of the same sewing-machine and lawn-mower—I felt as if I had been made free of the secrets of every village in every State of the Union, and as if I had lived in every little house and cottage thereof all my life! Almost no sense of beauty in those tremendous supplies of merchandise, but a lot of honesty, self-respect, and ambition fulfilled. I tell you I could hear the engaged couples discussing ardently over the pages of the catalogue what manner of bedroom suite they would buy, and what design of sideboard. . . .

Finally, I arrived at the firm's private railway station, where a score or more trucks were being laden with the multifarious boxes, bales, and parcels, all to leave that evening for romantic destinations such as Oregon, Texas, and Wyoming. Yes, the package of the woman of Wyoming's desire would ultimately be placed somewhere in one of those trucks! It was going to start off toward her that very night!

Impressive as this establishment was, finely as it illustrated the national genius for organization, it yet lacked necessarily, on account of the nature of its activity, those outward phenomena of splendor which charm the stranger's eye in the great central houses of New York, and which seem designed to sum up all that is most characteristic and most dazzling in the business methods of the United States. These central houses are not soiled by the touch of actual merchandise. Nothing more squalid than ink ever enters their gates. They traffic with symbols only, and the symbols, no matter what they stand for, are never in themselves sordid. The men who have created these houses seem to have realized that, from their situation and their importance, a special effort toward representative magnificence was their pleasing duty, and to have made the effort with a superb prodigality and an astounding ingenuity.

Take, for a good, glorious example, the very large insurance company, conscious that the eyes of the world are upon it, and that the entire United States is expecting it to uphold the national pride. All the splendors of all the sky-scrapers are united in its building. Its foyer and grand staircase will sustain comparison with those of the Paris Opéra. You might think you were going into a place of entertainment! And, as a fact, you are! This affair, with nearly four thousand clerks, is the huge toy and pastime of a group of millionaires who have discovered a way of honestly amusing themselves while gaining applause and advertisement. Within the foyer and beyond the staircase, notice the outer rooms, partitioned off by bronze grilles, looming darkly gorgeous in an eternal windowless twilight studded with the beautiful glowing green disks of electric-lamp shades; and under each disk a human head bent over the black-and-red magic of ledgers! The desired effect is at once obtained, and it is wonderful. Then lose yourself in and out of the ascending and descending elevators, and among the unending multitudes of clerks, and along the corridors of marble (total length exactly measured and recorded). You will be struck dumb. And immediately you begin to recover your speech you will be struck dumb again. . . .

Other houses, as has been seen, provide good meals for their employees at cost price. This house, then, will provide excellent meals, free of charge! It will install the most expensive kitchens and richly spacious restaurants. It will serve the delicate repasts with dignity. "Does all this lessen the wages?" No, not in theory. But in practice, and whether the management wishes or not, it must come out of the wages. "Why do you do it?" you ask the departmental chief, who apparently gets far more fun out of the contemplation of these refectories than out of the contemplation of premiums received and claims paid. "It is better for the employees," he says. "But we do it because it is better for us. It pays us. Good food, physical comfort, agreeable environment, scientific ventilation—all these things pay us. We get results from them." He does not mention horses, but you feel that the comparison is with horses. A horse, or a clerk, or an artisan—it pays equally well to treat all of them well. This is one of the latest discoveries of economic science, a discovery not yet universally understood.

I say you do not mention horses, and you certainly must not hint that the men in authority may have been actuated by motives of humanity. You must believe what you are told—that the sole motive is to get results. The eagerness with which all heads of model establishments would disavow to me any thought of being humane was affecting in its *naïveté;* it had that touch of ingenuous wistfulness which I remarked everywhere in America—and nowhere more than in the demeanor of many mercantile highnesses. (I hardly expect Americans to understand just what I mean here.) It was as if they would blush at being caught in an act of

A YOUNG WOMAN WAS JUST FINISHING A FLORID SONG

humanity, like school-boys caught praying. Still, to my mind, the white purity of their desire to get financial results was often muddied by the dark stain of a humane motive. I may be wrong (as people say), but I know I am not (as people think).

The further you advance into the penetralia of this arch-exemplar of American organization and profusion, the more you are amazed by the imaginative perfection of its detail: as well in the system of filing for instant reference fifty million separate documents, as in the planning of a concert-hall for the diversion of the human machines.

As we went into the immense concert-hall a group of girls were giving an informal concert among themselves. When lunch is served on the premises with chronographic exactitude, the thirty-five minutes allowed for the meal give an appreciable margin for music and play. A young woman was just finishing a florid song. The concert was suspended, and the whole party began to move humbly away at this august incursion.

"Sing it again; do, please!" the departmental chief suggested. And the florid song was nervously sung again; we applauded, the artiste bowed as on a stage, and the group fled, the thirty-five minutes being doubt-less up. The departmental chief looked at me in silence, content, as much as to say: "This is how we do business in America." And I thought, "Yet another way of getting results!"

But sometimes the creators of the organization, who had provided everything, had been obliged to confess that they had omitted from their designs certain factors of evolution. Hat-cupboards were a feature of the women's offices—delightful specimens of sound cabinetry. And still, millinery was lying about all over the place, giving it an air of feminine occupation that was extremely exciting to a student on his travels. The truth was that none of those hats would go into the cupboards. Fashion had worsted the organization completely. Departmental chiefs had nothing to bo but acquiesce in this startling untidiness. Either they must wait till the circumference of hats lessened again, or they must tear down the whole structure and rebuild it with due regard to hats.

Finally, we approached the sacred lair and fastness of the president, whose massive portrait I had already seen on several walls. Spaciousness and magnificence increased. Ceilings rose in height, marble was softened by the thick pile of carpets. Mahogany and gold shone more luxuriously. I was introduced into the vast antechamber of the presidential secretaries, and by the chief of them inducted through polished and gleaming barriers into the presence-chamber itself: a noble apartment, an apartment surpassing dreams and expectations, conceived and executed in a spirit of majestic prodigality. The president had not been afraid. And his costly audacity was splendidly justified of itself. This man had a sense of the romantic, of the dramatic, of the fit. And the qualities in him and his *état major* which had commanded the success of the entire enterprise were well shown in the brilliant symbolism of that room's grandiosity. . . . And there was the president's portrait again, gorgeously framed.

He came in through another door, an old man of superb physique, and after a little while he was relating to me the early struggles of his company. "My wife used to say that for ten years she never saw me," he remarked.

I asked him what his distractions were, now that the strain was over and his ambitions so gloriously achieved. He replied that occasionally he went for a drive in his automobile.

"And what do you do with yourself in the evenings?" I inquired.

He seemed a little disconcerted by this perhaps unaccustomed bluntness.

"Oh," he said, casually, "I read insurance literature."

He had the conscious mien and manners of a reigning prince. His courtesy and affability were impeccable and charming. In the most profound sense this human being had succeeded, for it was impossible to believe that, had he to live his life again, he would live it very differently.

Such a type of man is, of course, to be found in nearly every country; but the type flourishes with a unique profusion and perfection in the United States; and in its more prominent specimens the distinguishing idiosyncrasy of the average American successful man of business is magnified for our easier inspection. The rough, broad difference between the American and the European business man is that the latter is anxious to leave his work, while the former is anxious to get to it. The attitude of the American business man toward his business is pre-eminently the attitude of an artist. You may say that he loves money. So do we all—artists particularly. No stock-broker's private journal could be more full of dollars than Balzac's intimate correspondence is full of francs. But whereas the ordinary artist loves money chiefly because it represents luxury, the American business man loves it chiefly because it is the sole proof of success in his endeavor. He loves his business. It is not his toil, but his hobby, passion, vice, monomania—any vituperative epithet you like to bestow on it! He does not look forward to living in the evening; he lives most intensely when he is in the midst of his organization. His instincts are best appeased by the hourly excitements of a good, scrimmaging commercial day. He needs these excitements as some natures need alcohol. He cannot do without them.

On no other hypothesis can the unrivaled ingenuity and splendor and ruthlessness of American business undertakings be satisfactorily explained. They surpass the European, simply because they are never out of the thoughts of their directors, because they are adored with a fine frenzy. And for the same reason they are decked forth in magnificence. Would a man enrich his office with rare woods and stuffs and marbles if it were not a temple? Would he bestow graces on the environment if while he was in it the one idea at the back of his head was the anticipation of leaving it? Watch American business men together, and if you are a European you will clearly perceive that they are devotees. They are open with one another, as intimates are. Jealousy and secretiveness are much rarer among them than in Europe. They show off their respective

ABSORBED IN THAT WONDROUS SATISFYING HOBBY

organizations with pride and with candor. They admire one another enormously. Hear one of them say enthusiastically of another: "It was a great idea he had —connecting his New York and his Philadelphia places by wireless—a great idea!" They call one another by their Christian names, fondly. They are capable of wonderful friendships in business. They are cemented by one religion—and it is not golf. For them the journey "home" is often not the evening journey, but the morning journey. Call this a hard saying if you choose: it is true. Could a man be happy long away from a hobby so entrancing, a toy so intricate and marvelous, a setting so splendid? Is it strange that, absorbed in that wondrous satisfying hobby, he should make love with the nonchalance of an animal? At which point I seem to have come dangerously near to the topic of the singular position of the American woman, about which everybody is talking. . . .

V

TRANSIT AND HOTELS

V

TRANSIT AND HOTELS

THE choice of such a trite topic as the means of travel may seem to denote that my observations in the United States must have been superficial. They were. I never hoped that they would be otherwise. In seven weeks (less one day) I could not expect to penetrate very far below the engaging surface of things. Nor did I unnaturally attempt to do so; for the evidence of the superficies is valuable, and it can only be properly gathered by the stranger at first sight. Among the scenes and phenomena that passed before me I of course remember best those which interested me most. Railroads and trains have always appealed to me; I have often tried to express my sense of their romantic savor. And I was eager to see and appreciate these particular manifestations of national character in America.

It happily occurred that my first important journey from New York was on the Pennsylvania Road.

"I'll meet you at the station," I said to my particular friend.

"Oh no!" he answered, positively. "I'll pick you up on my way."

The fact was that not for ten thousand dollars would he have missed the spectacle of my sensations as I beheld for the first time the most majestic terminus in the world! He alone would usher me into the gates of that marvel! I think he was not disappointed. I frankly surrendered myself to the domination of this extraordinary building. I did not compare. I knew there could be no comparison. Whenever afterward I heard, as I often did, enlightened, Europe-loving citizens of the United States complain that the United States was all very well, but there was no art in the United States, the image of this tremendous master-piece would rise before me, and I was inclined to say: "Have you ever crossed Seventh Avenue, or are you merely another of those who have been to Europe and learned nothing?" The Pennsylvania station is full of the noble qualities that fine and heroic imagination alone can give. That there existed a railroad man poetic and audacious enough to want it, architects with genius powerful enough to create it, and a public with heart enough to love it—these things are for me a surer proof that the American is a great race than the exis-tence of any quantity of wealthy universities, museums of classic art, associations for prison reform, or deep-delved safe-deposit vaults crammed with bonds. Such a monument does not spring up by chance; it is part of the slow flowering of a nation's secret spirit!

The terminus emerged brilliantly from an examina-tion of the complicated detail, both esthetic and prac-tical, that is embedded in the apparent simplicity of its vast physiognomy. I discovered everything in it proper to a station, except trains. Not a sign of a train. My impulse was to ask, "Is this the tomb of Alexander J. Cassatt, or is it a cathedral, or is it, after all, a railroad

IN THE PARLOR-CAR

station?" Then I was led with due ceremony across the boundless plains of granite to a secret staircase, guarded by lions in uniform, and at the foot of this staircase, hidden like a shame or a crime, I found a resplendent train, the Congressional Limited. It was not the Limited of my dreams; but it was my first American Limited, and I boarded it in a condition of excitement. I criticized, of course, for every experienced traveler has decided views concerning *trains de luxe*. The cars impressed rather than charmed me. I preferred, and still prefer, the European variety of Pullman. (Yes, I admit we owe it entirely to America!) And then there is a harsh, inhospitable quality about those all-steel cars. They do not yield. You think you are touching wood, and your knuckles are abraded. The imitation of wood is a triumph of mimicry, but by no means a triumph of artistic propriety. Why should steel be made to look like wood? . . . Fireproof, you say. But is anything fireproof in the United States, except perhaps Tammany Hall? Has not the blazing of fireproof constructions again and again singed off the eyebrows of dauntless firemen? My impression is that "fireproof," in the American tongue, is one of those agreeable but quite meaningless phrases whch adorn the languages of all nations. Another such phrase, in the American tongue, is "right away!" . . .

I sat down in my appointed place in the all-steel car, and, turning over the pages of a weekly paper, saw photographs of actual collisions, showing that in an altercation between trains the steel-and-wood car could knock the all-steel car into a cocked hat! . . . The dec-

oration of the all-steel car does not atone for its prob-
able combustibility and its proved fragility. In particular, the smoking-cars of all the Limiteds I intrusted
myself to were defiantly and wilfully ugly. Still, a
fine, proud train, handsome in some ways! And the
trainmen were like admirals, captains, and first officers
pacing bridges; clearly they owned the train, and had
kindly lent it to the Pennsylvania R. R. Their demeanor
expressed a rare sense of ownership and also of responsibility. While very polite, they condescended.
A strong contrast to the miserable European "guard"
—for all his silver buttons! I adventured into the observation-car, of which institution I had so often heard
Americans speak with pride, and speculated why, here
as in all other cars, the tops of the windows were so low
that it was impossible to see the upper part of the
thing observed (roofs, telegraph-wires, tree-foliage, hill-
summits, sky) without bending the head and cricking
the neck. I do not deny that I was setting a high standard of perfection, but then I had heard so much all
my life about American Limiteds!

The Limited started with exactitude, and from the
observation-car I watched the unrolling of the wondrous
Hudson tunnel—one of the major sights of New York,
and a thing of curious beauty. . . . The journey passed
pleasantly, with no other episode than that of dinner,
which cost a dollar and was worth just about a dollar,
despite the mutton. And with exactitude we arrived
at Washington—another splendid station. I generalized
thus: "It is certain that this country understands railroad stations." I was, however, fresh in the country,

and had not then seen New Haven station, which, as soon as it is quite done with, ought to be put in a museum.

We returned from Washington by a night train; we might have taken a day train, but it was pointed out to me that I ought to get into "form" for certain projected long journeys into the West. At midnight I was brusquely introduced to the American sleeping-car. I confess that I had not imagined anything so appalling as the confined, stifling, malodorous promiscuity of the American sleeping-car, where men and women are herded together on shelves under the drastic control of an official aided by negroes. I care not to dwell on the subject. . . . I have seen European prisons, but in none that I have seen would such a system be tolerated, even by hardened warders and governors; and assuredly, if it were, public opinion would rise in anger and destroy it. I have not been in Siberian prisons, but I remember reading George Kennan's description of their mild horrors, and I am surprised that he should have put himself to the trouble of such a tedious journey when he might have discovered far more exciting material on any good road around New York. However, nobody seemed to mind, such is the force of custom—and I did not mind very much, because my particular friend, intelligently foreseeing my absurd European prejudices, had engaged for us a state-room.

This state-room, or suite—for it comprised two apartments—was a beautiful and aristocratic domain. The bedchamber had a fan that would work at three speeds like an automobile, and was an enchanting toy. In short, I could find no fault with the accommodation. It was perfect, and would have remained perfect had the train remained in the station. Unfortunately, the engine-driver had the unhappy idea of removing the train from the station. He seemed to be an angry engine-driver, and his gesture was that of a man setting his teeth and hissing: "Now, then, come out of that, you sluggards!" and giving a ferocious tug. There was a fearful jerk, and in an instant I understood why sleeping-berths in America are always arranged lengthwise with the train. If they were not, the passengers would spend most of the night in getting up off the floor and climbing into bed again. A few hundred yards out of the station the engine-driver decided to stop, and there was the same fearful jerk and concussion. Throughout the night he stopped and he started at frequent intervals, and always with the fearful jerk. Sometimes he would slow down gently and woo me into a false tranquillity, but only to finish with the same jerk rendered more shocking by contrast.

The bedchamber was delightful, the lavatory amounted to a boudoir, the reading-lamp left nothing to desire, the ventilation was a continuous vaudeville entertainment, the watch-pocket was adorable, the mattress was good. Even the road-bed was quite respectable—not equal to the best I knew, probably, but it had the great advantage of well-tied rails, so that as the train passed from one rail-length to the next you felt no jar, a bliss utterly unknown in Europe. The secret of a satisfactory "sleeper," however, does not lie in the stateroom, nor in the glittering lavatory, nor in the lamp.

nor in the fan, nor in the watch-pocket, nor in the bed, nor even in the road-bed. It lies in the mannerisms of that brave fellow out there in front of you on the engine, in the wind and the rain. But no one in all America seemed to appreciate this deep truth. For myself, I was inclined to go out to the engine-driver and say to him: "Brother, are you aware—you cannot be—that the best European trains start with the imperceptible stealthiness of a bad habit, so that it is impossible to distinguish motion from immobility, and come to rest with the softness of doves settling on the shoulders of a young girl?" . . . If the fault is not the engine-driver's, then are the brakes to blame? Inconceivable! . . . All American engine-drivers are alike; and I never slept a full hour in any American "sleeper," what with stops, starts, hootings, tollings, whizzings round sharp corners, listening to the passage of freight-trains, and listening to haughty conductor-admirals who quarreled at length with newly arrived voyagers at 2 or 3 A.M.! I do not criticize; I state. I also blame myself. There are those who could sleep. But not everybody could sleep. Well and heartily do I remember the moment when another friend of mine, in the midst of an interminable scolding that was being given by a nasal-voiced conductor to a passenger just before the dawn, exposed his head and remarked: "Has it occurred to you that this is a sleeping-car?" In the swift silence the whirring of my private fan could be heard.

I arrived in New York from Washington, as I arrived at all my destinations after a night journey, in a state of enfeebled submissiveness, and I retired to bed in a hotel.

And for several hours the hotel itself would stop and start with a jerk and whiz round corners.

—

For many years I had dreamed of traveling by the great, the unique, the world-renowned New York-Chicago train; indeed, it would not be a gross exaggeration to say that I came to America in order to take that train; and at length time brought my dream true. I boarded the thing in New York, this especial product of the twentieth century, and yet another thrilling moment in my life came and went! I boarded it with pride; everybody boarded it with pride; and in every eye was the gleam: "This is the train of trains, and I have my state-room on it." Perhaps I was ever so slightly disappointed with the dimensions and appointments of the state-room—I may have been expecting a whole car to myself—but the general self-conscious smartness of the train reassured me. I wandered into the observation-car, and saw my particular friend proudly employ the train-telephone to inform his office that he had caught the train. I saw also the free supply of newspapers, the library of books, the typewriting-machine, and the stenographer by its side—all as promised. And I knew that at the other end of the train was a dining-car, a smoking-car, and a barber-shop. I picked up the advertising literature scattered about by a thoughtful Company, and learned therefrom that this train was not a mere experiment; it was the finished fruit of many experiments, and that while offering the conveniences of a hotel or a club, it did with regularity

what it undertook to do in the way of speed and prompt-
ness. The pamphlet made good reading! . . .

I noted that it pleased the Company to run two other
very important trains out of the terminus simultaneously
with the unique train. Bravado, possibly; but bravado
which invited the respect of all those who admire enterprise! I anticipated with pleasure the noble spectacle
of these three trains sailing forth together on three
parallel tracks; which pleasure was denied me. We for
Chicago started last; we started indeed, according to
my poor European watch, from fifteen to thirty seconds
late! . . . No matter! I would not stickle for seconds:
particularly as at Chicago, by the terms of a contract
which no company in Europe would have had the grace
to sign, I was to receive, for any unthinkable lateness,
compensation at the rate of one cent for every thirty-
six seconds!

Within a quarter of an hour it became evident that
that train had at least one great quality—it moved.
As, in the deepening dusk, we swung along the banks of
the glorious Hudson, veiled now in the vaporous mys-
teries following a red sunset, I was obliged to admit
with increasing enthusiasm that that train did move.
Even the persecutors of Galileo would never have had
the audacity to deny that that train moved. And one
felt, comfortably, that the whole Company, with all
the Company's resources, was watching over its flying
pet, giving it the supreme right of way and urging it
forward by hearty good-will. One felt also that the
moment had come for testing the amenities of the hotel
and the club.

"Tea, please," I said, jauntily, confidently, as we entered the spotless and appetizing restaurant-car.

The extremely polite and kind captain of the car was obviously taken aback. But he instinctively grasped that the reputation of the train hung in the balance, and he regained his self-possession.

"Tea?" His questioning inflection delicately hinted: "Try not to be too eccentric."

"Tea."

"Here?"

"Here."

"I can serve it here, of course," said the captain, persuasively. "But if you don't mind I should prefer to serve it in your state-room."

We reluctantly consented. The tea was well made and well served.

In an instant, as it seemed, we were crossing a dark river, on which reposed several immense, many-storied river-steamers, brilliantly lit. I had often seen illustrations of these craft, but never before the reality. A fine sight—and it made me think of Mark Twain's incomparable masterpiece, *Life on the Mississippi*, for which I would sacrifice the entire works of Thackeray and George Eliot. We ran into a big town, full of electric signs, and stopped. Albany! One minute late! I descended to watch the romantic business of changing engines. I felt sure that changing the horses of a fashionable mail-coach would be as nothing to this. The first engine had already disappeared. The new one rolled tremendous and overpowering toward me; its wheels rose above my head, and the driver glanced down

BREAKFAST EN ROUTE

at me as from a bedroom window. I was sensible of all
the mystery and force of the somber monster; I felt the
mystery of the unknown railway station, and of the
strange illuminated city beyond. And I had a corner
in my mind for the thought: "Somewhere near me
Broadway actually ends." Then, while dark men under
the ray of a lantern fumbled with the gigantic couplings,
I said to myself that if I did not get back to my car I
should probably be left behind. I regained my state-
room and waited, watch in hand, for the jerk of restart-
ing. I waited half an hour. Some mishap with the
couplings! We left Albany thirty-three minutes late.
Habitués of the train affected nonchalance. One of
them offered to bet me that "she would make it up."
The admirals and captains avoided our gaze.

We dined, *à la carte;* the first time I had ever dined
à la carte on any train. An excellent dinner, well and
sympathetically served. The mutton was impeccable.
And in another instant, as it seemed, we were running,
with no visible flags, through an important and showy
street of a large town, and surface-cars were crossing
one another behind us. I had never before seen an
express train let loose in the middle of an unprotected
town, and I was *naïf* enough to be startled. But a
huge electric sign — "Syracuse bids you welcome" —
tranquilized me. We briefly halted, and drew away
from the allurement of those bright streets into the
deep, perilous shade of the open country.

I went to bed. The night differed little from other
nights spent in American sleeping-cars, and I therefore
will not describe it in detail. To do so might amount

YOUR UNITED STATES

to a solecism. Enough to say that the jerkings were possibly less violent and certainly less frequent than usual, while, on the other hand, the halts were strangely long; one, indeed, seemed to last for hours; I had to admit to myself that I had been to sleep and dreamed this stoppage.

From a final cat-nap I at last drew up my blind to greet the oncoming day, and was rewarded by one of the finest and most poetical views I have ever seen: a misty, brown river flanked by a jungle of dark reddish and yellowish chimneys and furnaces that covered it with shifting canopies of white steam and of smoke, varying from the delicatest grays to intense black; a beautiful dim gray sky lightening, and on the ground and low, flat roofs a thin crust of snow: Toledo! A wonderful and inspiring panorama, just as romantic in its own way as any Spanish Toledo. Yet I regretted its name, and I regretted the grotesque names of other towns on the route—Canaan, Syracuse, Utica, Geneva, Ceylon, Waterloo, and odd combinations ending in "burg." The names of most of the States are superb. What could be more beautiful than Ohio, Idaho, Kentucky, Iowa, Missouri, Wyoming, Illinois—above all, Illinois? Certain cities, too, have grand names. In its vocal quality "Chicago" is a perfect prince among names. But the majority of town names in America suffer, no doubt inevitably, from a lack of imagination and of reflection. They have the air of being bought in haste at a big advertising "ready-for-service" establishment.

Remembering in my extreme prostration that I was in a hotel and club, and not in an experiment, I rang

110

the bell, and a smiling negro presented himself. It was only a quarter to seven in Toledo, but I was sustained in my demeanor by the fact that it was a quarter to eight in New York.

"Will you bring me some tea, please?"

He was sympathetic, but he said flatly I couldn't have tea, nor anything, and that nobody could have anything at all for an hour and a half, as there would be no restaurant-car till Elkhart, and Elkhart was quite ninety miles off. He added that an engine had broken down at Cleveland.

I lay in collapse for over an hour, and then, summoning my manhood, arose. On the previous evening the hot-water tap of my toilette had yielded only cold water. Not wishing to appear hypercritical, I had said nothing, but I had thought. I now casually turned on the cold-water tap and was scalded by nearly boiling water. The hot-water tap still yielded cold water. Lest I should be accused of inventing this caprice of plumbing in a hotel and club, I give the name of the car. It was appropriately styled "Watertown" (compartment E).

In the corridor an admiral, audaciously interrogated, admitted that the train was at that moment two hours and ten minutes late. As for Elkhart, it seemed to be still about ninety miles away. I went into the observation-saloon to cheer myself up by observing, and was struck by a chill, and by the chilly, pinched demeanor of sundry other passengers, and by the apologetic faces of certain captains. Already in my state-room my senses had suspected a chill; but I had refused to believe my senses. I knew and had known all my life

that American trains were too hot, and I had put down
the supposed chill to a psychological delusion. It was,
however, no delusion. As we swept through a snowy
landscape the apologetic captains announced sadly that
the engine was not sparing enough steam to heat the
whole of the train. We put on overcoats and stamped
our feet.

The train was now full of ravening passengers. And
as Elkhart with infinite shyness approached, the ravening passengers formed in files in the corridors, and their
dignity was jerked about by the speed of the icy train,
and they waited and waited, like mendicants at the
kitchen entrance of a big restaurant. And at long last,
when we had ceased to credit that any such place as
Elkhart existed, Elkhart arrived. Two restaurant-cars
were coupled on, and, as it were, instantly put to the
sack by an infuriated soldiery. The food was excellent,
and newspapers were distributed with much generosity,
but some passengers, including ladies, had to stand for
another twenty minutes famished at the door of the
first car, because the breakfasting accommodation of
this particular hotel and club was not designed on the
same scale as its bedroom accommodation. We reached
Chicago one hundred and ten minutes late. And to
compensate me for the lateness, and for the refrigera-
tion, and for the starvation, and for being forced to eat
my breakfast hurriedly under the appealing, reproach-
ful gaze of famishing men and women, an official at the
Lasalle station was good enough to offer me a couple
of dollars. I accepted them. . . .

An unfortunate accident, you say. It would be more

IN THE SUBWAY ONE ENCOUNTERS AN INSISTENT, HURRYING STREAM

proper to say a series of accidents. I think "the greatest train in the world" is entitled to one accident, but not to several. And when, in addition to being a train, it happens to be a hotel and club, and not an experiment, I think that a system under which a serious breakdown anywhere between Syracuse and Elkhart (about three-quarters of the entire journey) is necessarily followed by starvation—I think that such a system ought to be altered—by Americans. In Europe it would be allowed to continue indefinitely.

Beyond question my experience of American trains led me to the general conclusion that the best of them were excellent. Nevertheless, I saw nothing in the organization of either comfort, luxury, or safety to justify the strange belief of Americans that railroad traveling in the United States is superior to railroad traveling in Europe. Merely from habit, I prefer European trains on the whole. It is perhaps also merely from habit that Americans prefer American trains.

As regards methods of transit other than ordinary railroad trains, I have to admit a certain general disappointment in the United States. The Elevated systems in the large cities are the terrible result of an original notion which can only be called unfortunate. They must either depopulate the streets through which they run or utterly destroy the sensibility of the inhabitants; and they enormously increase and complicate the dangers of the traffic beneath them. Indeed, in the view of the unaccustomed stranger, every Elevated is an affliction so appallingly hideous that no degree of convenience could atone for its horror. The New York Subway is a masterpiece of celerity, and in other ways less evil than an Elevated, but in the minimum decencies of travel it appeared to me to be inferior to several similar systems in Europe.

The surface-cars in all the large cities that I saw were less smart and less effective than those in sundry European capitals. In Boston particularly I cannot forget the excessive discomfort of a journey to Cambridge, made in the company of a host who had a most beautiful house, and who gave dinners of the last refinement, but who seemed unaccountably to look on the car journey as a sort of pleasant robustious outing. Nor can I forget—also in Boston—the spectacle of the citizens of Brookline—reputed to be the wealthiest suburb in the world—strap-hanging and buffeted and flung about on the way home from church, in surface-cars which really did carry inadequacy and brutality to excess.

The horse-cabs of Chicago had apparently been imported second-hand immediately after the great fire from minor towns in Italy.

There remains the supreme mystery of the vices of the American taxicab. I sought an explanation of this from various persons, and never got one that was convincing. The most frequent explanation, at any rate in New York, was that the great hotels were responsible for the vices of the American taxicab, by reason of their alleged outrageous charges to the companies for the privilege of waiting for hire at their august porticos. I listened with respect, but with incredulity. If the

THE STRAP-HANGERS

taxicabs were merely very dear, I could understand; if they were merely very bad, I could understand; if they were merely numerically insufficient for the number of people willing to pay for taxicabs, I could understand. But that they should be at once very dear, very bad, and most inconveniently scarce, baffled and still baffles me. The sum of real annoyance daily inflicted on a rich and busy but craven-hearted city like New York by the eccentricity of its taxicab organization must be colossal.

As to the condition of the roadways, the vocabulary of blame had been exhausted long before I arrived. Two things, however, struck me in New York which I had not heard of by report: the greasiness of the streets, transforming every automobile into a skidding death-trap at the least sign of moisture, and the leisureliness of the road-works. The busiest part of Thirty-fourth Street, for example—no mean artery, either—was torn up when I came into New York, and it was still torn up when I left. And, lastly, why are there no island refuges on Fifth Avenue? Even at the intersection of Fifth and Broadway there is no oasis for the pursued wayfarer. Every European city has long ago decided that the provision of island refuges in main thoroughfares is an act of elementary justice to the wayfarer in his unequal and exhausting struggle with wheeled traffic.

All these criticisms, which are severe but honest, would lose much of their point if the general efficiency of the United States and its delightful genius for organization were not so obvious and so impressive to the European. In fact, it is precisely the brilliant practical qualities of the country which place its idiosyncrasies in the matter of transit in so startling a light. . . . I would not care to close this section without a grateful reference to the very natty electric coupés, usually driven by ladies, which are so refreshing a feature of the streets of Chicago, and to the virtues of American private automobiles in general.

It is remarkable that a citizen who cheerfully and negligently submits to so many various inconveniences outside his home should insist on having the most comfortable home in the world, as the American citizen unquestionably has! Once, when in response to an interviewer I had become rather lyrical in praise of I forget what phenomenon in the United States, a Philadelphia evening newspaper published an editorial article in criticism of my views. This article was entitled "Offensive Flattery." Were I to say freely all that I thought of the American private house, large or small, I might expose myself again to the same accusation.

When I began to make the acquaintance of the American private house, I felt like one who, son of an exiled mother, had been born abroad and had at length entered his real country. That is to say, I felt at home. I felt that all this practical comfort and myself had been specially destined for each other since the beginning of time, and that fate was at last being fulfilled. Freely I admit that until I reached America I had not understood what real domestic comfort, generously conceived, could be. Certainly I had always in this particular quarreled with my own country, whose average notion

THE PASSENGERS ON THE ELEVATED AT NIGHT ARE ODDLY ASSORTED

of comfort still is to leave the drawing-room (temperature 70°—near the fire) at midnight, pass by a windswept hall and staircase (temperature 55°) to a bedroom full of fine fresh air (temperature 50° to 40°), and in that chamber, having removed piece by piece every bit of warm clothing, to slip, imperfectly protected, between icy sheets and wait for sleep. Certainly I had always contested the joyfulness of that particular process; but my imagination had fallen short of the delicious innumerable realities of comfort in an American home.

Now, having regained the "barbaric seats" whence I came, I read with a peculiar expression the advertisements of fashionable country and town residences to rent or for sale in England. Such as: "Choice residence. Five reception-rooms. Sixteen bedrooms. Bathroom—" Or: "Thoroughly up-to-date mansion. Six reception-rooms. Splendid hall. Billiard-room. Twenty-four bedrooms. Two bath-rooms—" I read this literature (to be discovered textually every week in the best illustrated weeklies), and I smile. Also I wonder, faintly blushing, what Americans truly *do* think of the residential aspects of European house-property when they first see it. And I wonder, without blushing, to what miraculous degree of perfected comfort Americans would raise all their urban traffic if only they cared enough to keep the professional politician out of their streets as strictly as they keep him out of their houses.

The great American hotel, too, is a wondrous haven for the European who in Europe has only tasted comfort in his dreams. The calm orderliness of the bed-

117

room floors, the adequacy of wardrobes and lamps, the
reckless profusion of clean linen, that charming notice
which one finds under one's door in the morning, "You
were called at seven-thirty, *and answered*," the funda-
mental principle that a bedroom without a bath-room
is not a bedroom, the magic laundry which returns your
effects duly starched in eight hours, the bells which are
answered immediately, the thickness of the walls, the
radiator in the elevator-shaft, the celestial invention of
the floor-clerk—I could catalogue the civilizing features
of the American hotel for pages. But the great American hotel is a classic, and to praise it may seem inept.
My one excuse for doing so is that I have ever been a
devotee of hotels, and once indeed wrote a whole book
about one. When I told the best interviewer in the
United States that my secret ambition had always been
to be the manager of a grand hotel, I was quite sincere.
And whenever I saw the manager of a great American
hotel traversing with preoccupied and yet aquiline glance
his corridors and public rooms, I envied him acutely.

The hospitality of those corridors and public rooms is
so wide and comprehensive that the ground floor and
mezzanine of a really big hotel in the United States offer
a spectacle of humanity such as cannot be seen in
Europe; they offer also a remarkable contrast to the
tranquillity of their own upper stories, where any eccentricity is vigorously discouraged. I think that it must
be the vast tumult and promiscuity of the ground floor
which is responsible for the relative inferiority of the
restaurant in a great American hotel. A restaurant
should be a paramount unit, but as a fact in these hotels

THE RESTAURANT OF A GREAT HOTEL IS BUT ONE FEATURE OF ITS
SPLENDOR

it is no more than an item in a series of resorts, several of which equal if they do not surpass it in popular interest. The Americans, I found, would show more interest in the barber-shop than in the restaurant. (And to see the American man of business, theoretically in a hurry, having his head bumped about by a hair-cutter, his right hand tended by one manicurist, his left hand tended by another manicurist, his boots polished by a lightning shiner, and his wits polished by the two manicurists together—the whole simultaneously—this spectacle in itself was possibly a reflection on the American's sense of proportion.) Further, a restaurant should be a sacred retreat, screened away from the world; which ideal is foreign to the very spirit of the great American hotel.

I do not complain that the representative celebrated restaurants fail to achieve an absolutely first-class cuisine. No large restaurant, either in the United States or out of it, can hope to achieve an absolutely first-class cuisine. The peerless restaurant is and must be a little one. Nor would I specially complain of the noise and thronging of the great restaurants, the deafening stridency of their music, the artistic violence of their decorations; these features of fashionable restaurants are now universal throughout the world, and the philosopher adapts himself to them. (Indeed, in favor of New York I must say that in one of the largest of its restaurants I heard a Chopin ballade well played on a good piano— and it was listened to in appreciative silence; event quite unique in my experience. Also, the large restaurant whose cuisine nearest approaches the absolutely first-class is in New York, and not in Europe.)

Nor would I complain that the waiter in the great restaurant neither understands English nor speaks a tongue which resembles English, for this characteristic, too, is very marked across the Atlantic. (One night, in a Boston hotel, after lingual difficulties with a head-waiter, I asked him in French if he was not French. He cuttingly replied in waiter's American: "I *was* French, but now I am an American." In another few years that man will be referring to Great Britain as "the old country.") . . .

No; what disconcerts the European in the great American restaurant is the excessive, the occasionally maddening slowness of the service, and the lack of interest in the service. Touching the latter defect, the waiter is not impolite; he is not neglectful. But he is, too often, passively hostile, or, at best, neutral. He, or his chief, has apparently not grasped the fact that buying a meal is not like buying a ton of coal. If the purchaser is to get value for his money, he must enjoy his meal; and if he is to enjoy the meal, it must not merely be efficiently served, but it must be efficiently served in a sympathetic atmosphere. The supreme business of a good waiter is to create this atmosphere. . . . True, that even in the country which has carried cookery and restaurants to loftier heights than any other—I mean, of course, Belgium, the little country of little restaurants—the subtle ether which the truly civilized diner demands is rare enough. But in the great restaurants of the great cities of America it is, I fancy, rarer than anywhere else.

VI

SPORT AND THE THEATER

VI

SPORT AND THE THEATER

I REMEMBER thinking, long before I came to the United States, at the time when the anti-gambling bill was a leading topic of American correspondence in European newspapers, that a State whose public opinion would allow even the discussion of a regulation so drastic could not possibly regard "sport" as sport is regarded in Europe. It might be very fond of gambling, but it could not be afflicted with the particular mania which in Europe amounts to a passion, if not to a religion. And when the project became law, and horse-racing was most beneficially and admirably abolished in the northeastern portion of the Republic, I was astonished. No such law could be passed in any European country that I knew. The populace would not suffer it; the small, intelligent minority would not care enough to support it; and the wealthy oligarchical priest-patrons of sport would be seriously convinced that it involved the ruin of true progress and the end of all things. Such is the sacredness of sport in Europe, where governments audacious enough to attack and overthrow the state-church have never dared to suggest the suppression of the vice by which alone the main form of sport lives. . . .

So that I did not expect to find the United States a

very "sporting" country. And I did not so find it.
I do not wish to suggest that, in my opinion, there is no
"sport" in the United States, but only that there is somewhat less than in Western Europe; as I have already
indicated, the differences between one civilization and
another are always slight, though they are invariably
exaggerated by rumor.

I know that the "sporting instinct"—a curious combination of the various instincts for fresh air, destruction, physical prowess, emulation, devotion, and betting
—is tolerably strong in America. I could name a list
of American sports as long as the list of dutiable articles
in the customs tariff. I am aware that over a million
golf balls are bought (and chiefly lost) in the United
States every year. I know that no residence there is
complete without its lawn-tennis court. I accept the
statement that its hunting is unequaled. I have admired the luxury and completeness of its country clubs.
Its yachting is renowned. Its horse-shows, to which en-
thusiasts repair in automobiles, are wondrous displays
of fashion. But none of these things is democratic;
none enters into the life of the mass of the people.
Nor can that fierce sport be called quite democratic
which depends exclusively upon, and is limited to, the
universities. A six-day cycling contest and a Presidential election are, of course, among the very greatest
sporting events in the world, but they do not occur
often enough to merit consideration as constant factors
of national existence.

Baseball remains a formidable item, yet scarcely capable of balancing the scale against the sports—football,

THE HORSE-SHOWS ARE WONDROUS DISPLAYS OF **FASHION**

cricket, racing, pelota, bull-fighting—which, in Europe, impassion the common people, and draw most of their champions from the common people. In Europe the advertisement hoardings—especially in the provinces—proclaim sport throughout every month of the year; not so in America. In Europe the most important daily news is still the sporting news, as any editor will tell you; not so in America, despite the gigantic headings of the evening papers at certain seasons.

But how mighty, nevertheless, is baseball! Its fame floats through Europe as something prodigious, incomprehensible, romantic, and terrible. After being entertained at early lunch in the correct hotel for this kind of thing, I was taken, in a state of great excitement, by a group of excited business men, and flashed through Central Park in an express automobile to one of the great championship games. I noted the excellent arrangements for dealing with feverish multitudes. I noted the splendid and ornate spaciousness of the grand-stand crowned with innumerable eagles, and the calm, matter-of-fact tone in which a friend informed me that the grand-stand had been burned down six months ago. I noted the dreadful prominence of advertisements, and particularly of that one which announced "the 3-dollar hat with the 5-dollar look," all very European! It was pleasant to be convinced in such large letters that even shrewd America is not exempt from that universal human naïveté which is ready to believe that in some magic emporium a philanthropist is always waiting to give five dollars' worth of goods in exchange for three dollars of money.

Then I braced my intelligence to an understanding of the game, which, thanks to its classical simplicity, and to some training in the finesse of cricket and football, I did soon grasp in its main outlines. A beautiful game, superbly played. We reckon to know something of ball games in Europe; we reckon to be connoisseurs; and the old footballer and cricketer in me came away from that immense inclosure convinced that baseball was a game of the very first class, and that those players were the most finished exponents of it. I was informed that during the winter the players condescended to follow the law and other liberal professions. But, judging from their apparent importance in the public eye, I should not have been surprised to learn that during the winter they condescended to be Speakers of the House of Representatives or governors of States. It was a relief to know that in the matter of expenses they were treated more liberally than the ambassadors of the Republic.

They seemed to have carried the art of pitching a ball to a more wondrous degree of perfection than it has ever been carried in cricket. The absolute certitude of the fielding and accuracy of the throwing was profoundly impressive to a connoisseur. Only in a certain lack of elegance in gesture, and in the unshaven dowdiness of the ground on which it was played, could this game be said to be inferior to the noble spectacle of cricket. In broad dramatic quality I should place it above cricket, and on a level with Association football.

In short, I at once became an enthusiast for baseball. For nine innings I watched it with interest unabated, until a vast purple shadow, creeping gradually eastward, had obscurely veiled the sublime legend of the 3-dollar hat with the 5-dollar look. I began to acquire the proper cries and shouts and menaces, and to pass comments on the play which I was assured were not utterly foolish. In my honest yearning to feel myself a habitué, I did what everybody else did and even attacked a morsel of chewing-gum; but all that a European can say of this singular substance is that it is, finally, eternal and unconquerable. One slip I did quite innocently make. I rose to stretch myself after the sixth inning instead of half-way through the seventh. Happily a friend with marked presence of mind pulled me down to my seat again, before I had had time fully to commit this horrible sacrilege. When the game was finished I surged on to the enormous ground, and was informed by inner-ring experts of a few of the thousand subtle tactical points which I had missed. And lastly, I was flung up onto the Elevated platform, littered with pieces of newspaper, and through a landscape of slovenly apartment-houses, punctuated by glimpses of tremendous quantities of drying linen, I was shot out of New York toward a calm week-end.

Yes, a grand game, a game entirely worthy of its reputation! If the professional matador and gladiator business is to be carried on at all, a better exemplification of it than baseball offers could hardly be found or invented. But the beholding crowd, and the behavior of the crowd, somewhat disappointed me. My friends said with intense pride that forty thousand persons were present. The estimate proved to be an exaggeration; but even had it not been, what is forty thousand to the similar crowds in Europe? In Europe forty thousand people will often assemble to watch an ordinary football match. And for a "Final," the record stands at something over a hundred thousand. It should be remembered, too, in forming the comparison, that many people in the Eastern States frequent the baseball grounds because they have been deprived of their horse-racing. Further, the New York crowd, though fairly excited, was not excited as sporting excitement is understood in, for instance, the Five Towns. The cheering was good, but it was not the cheering of frenzied passion. The anathemas, though hearty, lacked that religious sincerity which a truly sport-loving populace will always put into them. The prejudice in favor of the home team, the cruel, frank unfairness toward the visiting team, were both insufficiently accentuated. The menaces were merely infantile. I inquired whether the referee or umpire, or whatever the arbiter is called in America, ever went in danger of life or limb, or had to be protected from a homicidal public by the law in uniform. And I was shocked by a negative answer. Referees in Europe have been smuggled off the ground in the center of a cocoon of policemen, have even been known to spend a fortnight in bed, after giving a decision adverse to the home team! . . . More evidence that the United States is not in the full sense a sporting country!

Of the psychology of the great common multitude of baseball "bleachers," I learned almost nothing. But as regards the world of success and luxury (which, of course, held me a willing captive firmly in its soft and powerful influence throughout my stay), I should say that there was an appreciable amount of self - hypnotism in its attitude toward baseball. As if the thriving and preoccupied business man murmured to his soul, when the proper time came: "By the way, these baseball championships are approaching. It is right and good for me that I should be boyishly excited, and I will be excited. I must not let my interest in baseball die. Let's look at the sporting-page and see how things stand. And I'll have to get tickets, too!" Hence possibly what seemed to me a superficiality and factitiousness in the excitement of the more expensive seats, and a too-rapid effervescence and finish of the excitement when the game was over.

The high fever of inter-university football struck me as a more authentic phenomenon. Indeed, a university town in the throes of an important match offers a psychological panorama whose genuineness can scarcely be doubted. Here the young men communicate the sacred contagion to their elders, and they also communicate it to the young women, who, in turn, communicate it to the said elders—and possibly the indirect method is the surer! I visited a university town in order to witness a match of the highest importance. Unfortunately, and yet fortunately, my whole view of it was affected by a mere nothing—a trifle which the newspapers dealt with in two lines.

When I reached the gates of the arena in the morning, to get a glimpse of a freshmen's match, an automobile was standing thereat. In the automobile was a pile of rugs, and sticking out of the pile of rugs in an odd, unnatural, horizontal way was a pair of muddy football boots. These boots were still on the feet of a boy, but all the rest of his unconscious and smashed body was hidden beneath the rugs. The automobile vanished, and so did my peace of mind. It seemed to me tragic that that burly infant under the rugs should have been martyrized at a poor little morning match in front of a few sparse hundreds of spectators and tens of thousands of unresponsive empty benches. He had not had even the glory and meed of a great multitude's applause. When I last inquired about him, at the end of the day, he was still unconscious, and that was all that could be definitely said of him; one heard that it was his features that had chiefly suffered in the havoc, that he had been defaced. If I had not happened to see those muddy football boots sticking out, I should have heard vaguely of the accident, and remarked philosophically that it was a pity, but that accidents would occur, and there would have been the end of my impression. Only I just did happen to see those muddy boots sticking out.

When we came away from the freshmen's match, the charming roads of the town, bordered by trees and by the agreeable architecture of mysterious clubs, were beginning to be alive and dangerous with automobiles and carriages, and pretty girls and proud men, and flags and flowers, and colored favors and shoutings. Salutes were being exchanged at every yard. The sense of a mighty and culminating event sharpened the air. The great inn was full of jollity and excitement, and the reception-clerks thereof had the negligent mien of those who know

THE SENSE OF A MIGHTY AND CULMINATING EVENT SHARPENED THE AIR

that every bedroom is taken and every table booked. The club (not one of the mysterious ones, but an ingenuous plain club of patriarchs who had once been young in the university and were now defying time) was crammed with amiable confusion, and its rich carpets protected for the day against the feet of bald lads, who kept aimlessly walking up-stairs and down-stairs and from room to room, out of mere friendly exuberance.

And after the inn and the club I was conducted into a true American home, where the largest and most free hospitality was being practised upon a footing of universal intimacy. You ate standing; you ate sitting; you ate walking the length of the long table; you ate at one small table, and then you ate at another. You talked at random to strangers behind and strangers before. And when you couldn't think of anything to say, you just smiled inclusively. You knew scarcely anybody's name, but the heart of everybody. Impossible to be ceremonious! When a young woman bluntly inquired the significance of that far-away look in your eye, impossible not to reply frankly that you were dreaming of a second helping of a marvelous pie up there at the end of the long table; and impossible not to eat all the three separate second helpings that were instantly thrust upon you! The chatter and the good-nature were enormous. This home was an expression of the democracy of the university at its best. Fraternity was abroad; kindliness was abroad; and therefore joy. Whatever else was taught at the university, these were taught, and they were learnt. If a publicist asked me what American civilization had achieved, I would answer that among other things it had achieved this hour in this modest home.

Occasionally a face would darken and a voice grow serious, exposing the terrible secret apprehensions, based on expert opinion, that the home side could not win. But the cloud would pass. And occasionally there would be a reference to the victim whose muddy boots I had seen. "Dreadful, isn't it?" and a twinge of compassion for the victim or for his mother! But the cloud would immediately pass.

And then we all had to leave, for none must be late on this solemn and gay occasion. And now the roads were so many converging torrents of automobiles and carriages, and excitement had developed into fever. Life was at its highest, and the world held but one problem. . . . Sign that reaction was approaching!

A proud spectacle for the agitated vision, when the vast business of filling the stands had been accomplished, and the eye ranged over acres of black hats and variegated hats, hats flowered and feathered, and plain male caps—a carpet intricately patterned with the rival colors! At a signal the mimic battle began. And in a moment occurred the first casualty—most grave of a series of casualties. A pale hero, with a useless limb, was led off the field amid loud cheers. Then it was that I became aware of some dozens of supplementary heroes shivering beneath brilliant blankets under the lee of the stands. In this species of football every casualty was foreseen, and the rules allowed it to be repaired. Not two teams, but two regiments, were, in fact, fighting. And my European ideal of sport was offended.

SPORT AND THE THEATER

Was it possible that a team could be permitted to re-
place a wounded man by another, and so on *ad infinitum?*
Was it possible that a team need not abide by its mis-
fortunes? Well, it was! I did not like this. It seemed
to me that the organizers, forgetting that this was a
mimic battle, had made it into a real battle, and that
there was an imperfect appreciation of what strictly
amateur sport is. The desire to win, laudable and essential in itself, may by excessive indulgence become a
morbid obsession. Surely, I thought, and still think,
the means ought to suit the end! An enthusiast for
American organization, I was nevertheless forced to
conclude that here organization is being carried too far,
outraging the sense of proportion and of general fitness.
For me, such organization disclosed even a misappre-
hension as to the principal aim and purpose of a university. If ever the fate of the Republic should depend
on the result of football matches, then such organization would be justifiable, and courses of intellectual
study might properly be suppressed. Until that dread
hour I would be inclined to dwell heavily on the admitted fact that a football match is not Waterloo, but
simply a transient game in which two sets of youngsters
bump up against one another in opposing endeavors
to put a bouncing toy on two different spots of the
earth's surface. The ultimate location of the inflated
bauble will not affect the national destiny, and such
moral value as the game has will not be increased but
diminished by any enlargement of organization. After
all, if the brains of the world gave themselves exclusively to football matches, the efficiency of football matches

would be immensely improved—but what then? . . . I seemed to behold on this field the American passion for "getting results"—which I admire very much; but it occurred to me that that passion, with its eyes fixed hungrily on the result it wants, may sometimes fail to see that it is getting a number of other results which it emphatically doesn't want.

Another example of excessive organization presented itself to me in the almost military arrangements for shrieking the official yells. I was sorry for the young men whose duty it was, by the aid of megaphones and of grotesque and undignified contortions, to encourage and even force the spectators to emit in unison the complex noises which constitute the yell. I have no doubt that my pity was misdirected, for these young men were obviously content with themselves; still, I felt sorry for them. Assuming for an instant that the official yell is not monstrously absurd and surpassingly ugly, admitting that it is a beautiful series of sounds, enheartening, noble, an utterance worthy of a great and ancient university at a crisis, even then one is bound to remember that its essential quality should be its spontaneity. Enthusiasm cannot be created at the word of command, nor can heroes be inspired by cheers artificially produced under megaphonic intimidation. Indeed, no moral phenomenon could be less hopeful to heroes than a perfunctory response to a military order for enthusiasm. Perfunctory responses were frequent. Partly, no doubt, because the imperious young men with megaphones would not leave us alone. Just when we were nicely absorbed in the caprices of the ball they would call us

THE VICTORS LEAVING THE FIELD

off and compel us to execute their preposterous chorus; and we—the spectators—did not always like it.

And the difficulty of following the game was already acute enough! Whenever the play quickened in interest we stood up. In fact, we were standing up and sitting down throughout the afternoon. And as we all stood up and we all sat down together, nobody gained any advantage from these muscular exercises. We saw no better, and we saw no worse. Toward the end we stood on the seats, with the same result. We behaved in exactly the child-like manner of an Italian audience at a fashionable concert. And to crown all, an aviator had the ineffably bad taste and the culpable foolhardiness to circle round and round within a few dozen yards of our heads.

In spite of all this, the sum of one's sensations amounted to lively pleasure. The pleasure would have been livelier if university football were a better game than in candid truth it is. At this juncture I seem to hear a million voices of students and ex-students roaring out at me with menaces that the game is perfect and the greatest of all games. A national game always was and is perfect. This particular game was perfect years ago. Nevertheless, I learned that it had recently been improved, in deference to criticisms. Therefore, it is now pluperfect. I was told on the field—and sharply— that experience of it was needed for the proper appreciation of its finesse. Admitted! But just as devotees of a favorite author will put sublime significances into his least phrase, so will devotees of a game put marvels of finesse into its clumsiest features. The process is psychological. I was new to this particular game, but I had been following various footballs with my feet or with my eyes for some thirty years, and I was not to be bullied out of my opinion that the American university game, though goodish, lacked certain virtues. Its characteristics tend ever to a too close formation, and inevitably favor tedium and monotony. In some aspects an unemotional critic might occasionally be tempted to call it naïve and barbaric. But I was not unemotional. I recognize, and in my own person I proved, that as a vehicle for emotion the American university game will serve. What else is such a game for? In the match I witnessed there were some really great moments, and one or two masterly exhibitions of skill and force. And as "my" side won, against all odds, I departed in a state of felicity.

If the great cities of the East and Middle West are not strikingly sportive, perhaps the reason is that they are impassioned theater-goers; they could not well be both, at any rate without neglecting the financial pursuits which are their chief real amusement and hobby. I mention the theaters in connection with sports, rather than in connection with the arts, because the American drama is more closely related to sporting diversions than to dramatic art. If this seems a hard saying, I will add that I am ready to apply it with similiar force to the English and French drama, and, indeed, to almost all modern drama outside Germany. It was astonishing to me that America, unhampered by English traditions, should take seriously, for instance, the fashionable and

utterly meretricious French dramatists, who receive
nothing but a chilly ridicule from people of genuine
discrimination in Paris. Whatever American dramatists have to learn, they will not learn it in Paris; and
I was charmed once to hear a popular New York play-
wright, one who sincerely and frankly wrote for money
alone, assert boldly that the notoriously successful
French plays were bad, and clumsily bad. It was a
proof of taste. As a rule, one finds the popular play-
wright taking off his hat to contemporaries who at best
are no better than his equals.

A few minor cases apart, the drama is artistically
negligible throughout the world; but if there is a large
hope for it in any special country, that country is the
United States. The extraordinary prevalence of big
theaters, the quickly increasing number of native
dramatists, the enormous profits of the successful ones
—it is simply inconceivable in the face of the phenomena,
and of the educational process so rapidly going on, that
serious and first-class creative artists shall not arise in
America. Nothing is more likely to foster the production of first-class artists than the existence of a vast
machinery for winning money and glory. When I reflect that there are nearly twice as many first-class
theaters in New York as in London, and that a very
successful play in New York plays to eighteen thousand
dollars a week, while in London ten thousand dollars a
week is enormous, and that the American public has a
preference for its own dramatists, I have little fear for
the artistic importance of the drama of the future in
America. And from the discrepancy between my own

observations and the observations of a reliable European critic in New York only five years ago, I should imagine that appreciable progress had already been made, though I will not pretend that I was much impressed by the achievements up to date, either of playwrights, actors, or audiences. A huge popular institution, however, such as the American theatrical system, is always interesting to the amateur of human nature.

The first thing noted by the curious stranger in American theaters is that American theatrical architects have made a great discovery—namely, that every member of the audience goes to the play with a desire to be able to see and hear what passes on the stage. This happy American discovery has not yet announced itself in Europe, where in almost every theater seats are impudently sold, and idiotically bought, from which it is impossible to see and hear what passes on the stage. (A remarkable continent, Europe!) Apart from this most important point, American theaters are not, either without or within, very attractive. The auditoriums, to a European, have a somewhat dingy air. Which air is no doubt partly due to the non-existence of a rule in favor of evening dress (never again shall I gird against the rule in Europe!), but it is due also to the oddly inefficient illumination during the entr'actes, and to the unsatisfactory schemes of decoration.

The interior of a theater ought to be magnificent, suggesting pleasure, luxury, and richness; it ought to create an illusion of rather riotous grandeur. The rare architects who have understood this seem to have lost their heads about it, with such wild and capricious results as the new opera-house in Philadelphia. I could not restrain my surprise that the inhabitants of the Quaker City had not arisen with pickaxes and razed this architectural extravaganza to the ground. But Philadelphia is a city startlingly unlike its European reputation. Throughout my too-brief sojourn in it I did not cease to marvel at its liveliness. I heard more picturesque and pyrotechnic wit at one luncheon in Philadelphia than at any two repasts outside it. The spacious gaiety and lavishness of its marts enchanted me. It must have a pretty weakness for the most costly old books and manuscripts. I never was nearer breaking the Sixth Commandment than in one of its homes, where the Countess of Pembroke's own copy of Sir Philip Sidney's *Arcadia*—a unique and utterly un-Quakerish treasure— was laid trustfully in my hands by the regretted and charming Harry Widener.

To return. The Metropolitan Opera-House in New York is a much more satisfactory example of a theatrical interior. Indeed, it is very fine, especially when strung from end to end of its first tier with pearls, as I saw it. Impossible to find fault with its mundane splendor. And let me urge that impeccable mundane splendor, despite facile arguments to the contrary, is a very real and worthy achievement. It is regrettable, by the way, that the entrances and foyers to these grandiose interiors should be so paltry, slatternly, and inadequate. If the entrances to the great financial establishments reminded me of opera-houses, the entrances to opera-houses did not!

Artistically, of course, the spectacle of a grand-opera

season in an American city is just as humiliating as it is in the other Anglo-Saxon country. It was disconcerting to see Latin or German opera given exactly—with no difference at all; same Latin or German artists and conductors, same conventions, same tricks—in New York or Philadelphia as in Europe. And though the wealthy audiences behaved better than wealthy audiences at Covent Garden (perhaps because the boxes are less like inclosed pews than in London), it was mortifying to detect the secret disdain for art which was expressed in the listless late arrivings and the relieved early departures. The which disdain for art was, however, I am content to think, as naught in comparison with the withering artistic disdain felt, and sometimes revealed, by those Latin and German artists for Anglo-Saxon Philistinism. I seem to be able to read the sarcastic souls of these accomplished and sensitive aliens, when they assure newspaper reporters that New York, Chicago, Boston, Philadelphia, and London are really musical. The sole test of a musical public is that it should be capable of self-support—I mean that it should produce a school of creative and executive artists of its own, whom it likes well enough to idolize and to enrich, and whom the rest of the world will respect. This is a test which can be safely applied to Germany, Russia, Italy, and France. And in certain other arts it is a test which can be applied to Anglo-Saxondom—but not in music. In America and England music is still mainly a sportive habit.

When I think of the exoticism of grand opera in New York, my mind at once turns, in contrast, to the natural raciness of such modest creations as those offered by Mr. George Cohan at his theater on Broadway. Here, in an extreme degree, you get a genuine instance of a public demand producing the desired artist on the spot. Here is something really and honestly and respectably American. And why it should be derided by even the most lofty pillars of American taste, I cannot imagine. (Or rather, I can imagine quite well.) For myself, I spent a very agreeable evening in witnessing "The Little Millionaire." I was perfectly conscious of the blatancy of the methods that achieved it. I saw in it no mark of genius. But I did see in it a very various talent and an all-round efficiency; and, beneath the blatancy, an admirable direct simplicity and winning unpretentiousness. I liked the ingenuity of the device by which, in the words of the programme, the action of Act II was "not interrupted by musical numbers." The dramatic construction of this act was so consistently clever and right and effective that more ambitious dramatists might study it with advantage. Another point — though the piece was artistically vulgar, it was not vulgar otherwise. It contained no slightest trace of the outrageous salacity and sottishness which disfigure the great majority of successful musical comedies. It was an honest entertainment. But to me its chief value and interest lay in the fact that while watching it I felt that I was really in New York, and not in Vienna, Paris, or London.

Of the regular theater I did not see nearly enough to be able to generalize even for my own private satisfaction. I observed, and expected to observe, that the most reactionary quarters were the most respected. It is the same everywhere. When a manager, having discovered that two real clocks in one real room never strike simultaneously, put two real clocks on the stage, and made one strike after the other; or when a manager mimicked, with extraordinary effects of restlessness, a life-sized telephone-exchange on the stage—then was I bound to hear of "artistic realism" and "a fine production"! But such feats of truthfulness do not consort well with chocolate sentimentalities and wilful falsities of action and dialogue. They caused me to doubt whether I was not in London.

The problem-plays which I saw were just as futile and exasperating as the commercial English and French varieties of the problem-play, though they had a trifling advantage over the English in that their most sentimental passages were lightened by humor, and the odiously insincere felicity of their conclusions was left to the imagination instead of being acted ruthlessly out on the boards. The themes of these plays showed the usual obsession, and were manipulated in the usual attempt to demonstrate that the way of transgressors is not so very hard after all. They threw, all unconsciously, strange side-lights on the American man's private estimate of the American woman, and the incidence of the applause was extremely instructive.

The most satisfactory play that I saw, "Bought and Paid For," by George Broadhurst, was not a problem-play, though Mr. Broadhurst is also a purveyor of problem-plays. It was just an unpretentious fairy-tale about the customary millionaire and the customary poor girl.

The first act was maladroit, but the others made me think that "Bought and Paid For" was one of the best popular commercial Anglo-Saxon plays I had ever seen anywhere. There were touches of authentic realism at the very crisis at which experience had taught one to expect a crass sentimentality. The fairy-tale was well told, with some excellent characterization, and very well played. Indeed, Mr. Frank Craven's rendering of the incompetent clerk was a masterly and unforgettable piece of comedy. I enjoyed "Bought and Paid For," and it is on the faith of such plays, imperfect and timid as they are, that I establish my prophecy of a more glorious hereafter for the American drama.

VII

EDUCATION AND ART

VII

EDUCATION AND ART

I HAD my first glimpses of education in America from the purser of an illustrious liner, who affirmed the existence of a dog—in fact, his own dog—so highly educated that he habitually followed and understood human conversations, and that in order to keep secrets from the animal it was necessary to spell out the key-word of a sentence instead of pronouncing it. After this I seemed somehow to be prepared for the American infant who, when her parents discomfited her just curiosity by the same mean adult dodge of spelling words, walked angrily out of the room with the protest: "There's too blank much education in this house for me!" Nevertheless, she proudly and bravely set herself to learn to spell; whereupon her parents descended to even worse depths of baseness, and in her presence would actually whisper in each other's ear. She merely inquired, with grimness: "What's the good of being educated, anyway? First you spell words, and when I can spell then you go and whisper!" And received no adequate answer, naturally.

This captivating creature, whose society I enjoyed at frequent intervals throughout my stay in America, was a mirror in which I saw the whole American race of children—their independence, their self-confidence, their adorable charm, and their neat sauciness. "What *is* father?" she asked one day. Now her father happened to be one of the foremost humorists in the United States; she was baldly informed that he was a humorist. "What *is* a humorist?" she went on, ruthlessly, and learned that a humorist was a person who wrote funny things to make people laugh. "Well," she said, "I don't honestly think he's very funny at home." It was naught to her that humorists are not paid to be funny at home, and that in truth they never under any circumstances are very funny at home. She just hurled her father from his niche—and then went forth and boasted of him as a unique peculiarity in fathers, as an unrivaled ornament of her career on earth; for no other child in the vicinity had a professional humorist for parent. Her gestures and accent typified for me the general attitude of youngest America, in process of education, toward the older generation: an astonishing, amusing, exquisite, incomprehensible mixture of affection, admiration, trust, and rather casual tolerating scorn. The children of most countries display a similar phenomenon, but in America the phenomenon is more acute and disconcerting than elsewhere.

One noon, in perfect autumn weather, I was walking down the main road of a residential suburb, and observing the fragile-wheeled station-wagons, and the ice-wagons enormously labeled "DANGER" (perhaps by the gastric experts of the medical faculty), and the Colonial-style dwellings, and the "tinder" boarding-houses, and the towering boot-shine stands, and the roast-chestnut emporia, and the gasometers flanking a noble and beautiful river—I was observing all this when a number of young men and maids came out of a high-school and unconsciously assumed possession of the street. It was a great and impressive sight; it was a delightful sight. They were so sure of themselves, the maids particularly; so interested in themselves, so happy, so eager, so convinced (without any conceit) that their importance transcended all other importances, so gently pitiful toward men and women of forty-five, and so positive that the main function of elders was to pay school-fees, that I was thrilled thereby. Seldom has a human spectacle given me such exciting pleasure as this gave. (And they never suspected it, those preoccupied demigods!) It was the sheer pride of life that I saw passing down the street and across the badly laid tram-lines! I had never seen anything like it. I immediately desired to visit schools. Profoundly ignorant of educational methods, and with a strong distaste for teaching, I yet wanted to know and understand all about education in America in one moment— the education that produced that superb stride and carriage in the street! I failed, of course, in my desire— not from lack of facilities offered, but partly from lack of knowledge to estimate critically what I saw, and from lack of time. My experiences, however, though they left my mind full of enigmas, were wondrous. I asked to inspect one of the best schools in New York. Had I been a dispassionate sociological student, I should probably have asked to inspect one of the worst schools in New York—perhaps one of the gaunt institutions to be found, together with a cinema-palace and a bank, in al-

most every block on the East Side.   But I asked for one
of the best, and I was shown the Horace Mann School.

The Horace Mann School proved to be a palace where
a thousand children and their teachers lived with extreme vivacity in an atmosphere of ozone from which
all draughts and chilliness had been eliminated.   As a
malcontent native of the Isle of Chilly Draughts, this
attribute of the atmosphere of the Horace Mann School
impresssd me.   Dimensionally I found that the palace
had a beginning but no end.   I walked through leagues
of corridors and peeped into unnumbered class-rooms,
in each of which children were apparently fiercely dragging knowledge out of nevertheless highly communica-
tive teachers; and the children got bigger and bigger,
and then diminished for a while, and then grew again,
and kept on growing, until I at last entered a palatial
kitchen where some two dozen angels, robed in white
but for the moment uncrowned, were eagerly crowding
round a paradisiacal saucepan whose magic contents
formed the subject of a lecture by one of them.   Now
these angels were not cherubs; they were full grown;
they never would be any taller than they were; and I
asked up to what age angels were kept at school in
America.   Whereupon I learned that I had insensibly
passed from the school proper into a training-school for
teachers; but at what point the school proper ended I
never did learn.   It seems to me that if I had penetrated
through seven more doors I should have reached Columbia University itself, without having crossed a definite di-
viding-line; and, anyhow, the circumstance was symbolic.

EDUCATION AND ART

Reluctantly I left the incredible acres of technical apparatus munificently provided in America for the training of teachers, and, having risen to the roof and seen infants thereon grabbing at instruction in the New York breeze, I came again to the more normal regions of the school. Here, as everywhere else in the United States (save perhaps the cloak-room department of the Metropolitan Opera - House), what chiefly struck me was the brilliant organization of the organism. There was nothing that had not been thought of. A handsomely dressed mother came into the organism and got as far as the antechamber of the principal's room. The organization had foreseen her, had divined that that mother's child was the most important among a thousand children—indeed, the sole child of any real importance —had arranged that her progress should be arrested at just that stage, and had stationed a calm and diplomatic woman to convince her that her child was indeed the main preoccupation of the Horace Mann School. A pretty sight—the interview! It charmed me as the sight of an ingenious engine in motion will charm an engineer.

The individual class-rooms, in some of which I lingered at leisure, were tonic, bracing, inspiring, and made me ashamed because I was not young. I saw geography being taught with the aid of a stereoscopic magic-lantern. After a view of the high street of a village in North Russia had been exposed and explained by a pupil, the teacher said: "If anybody has any questions to ask, let him stand up." And the whole class leaped furious-ly to its feet, blotting out the entire picture with black shadows of craniums and starched pinafores. The whole class might have been famishing. In another room I saw the teaching of English composition. Although when I went to school English composition was never taught, I have gradually acquired a certain interest in the subject, and I feel justified in asserting that the lesson was admirably given. It was, in fact, the best example of actual pedagogy that I met with in the United States. "Now can any one tell me—" began the mistress. A dozen arms of boys and girls shot up with excessive violence, and, having shot up, they wiggled and waggled with ferocious impatience in the air; it was a miracle that they remained attached to their respective trunks; it was assuredly an act of daring on the part of the intrepid mistress to choose between them.

"How children have changed since my time!" I said to the principal afterward. "We never used to fling up our hands like that. We just put them up. . . . But perhaps it's because they're Americans—"

"It's probably because of the ventilation," said the principal, calmly corrective. "We never have the windows open winter or summer, but the ventilation is perfect."

I perceived that it indeed must be because of the ventilation.

More and more startled, as I went along, by the princely lavishness of every arrangement, I ventured to surmise that it must all cost a great deal.

"The fees are two hundred and eighty-five dollars in the Upper School."

"Yes, I expected they would be high," I said.

"Not at all. They are the lowest in New York. Smart private schools will charge five or six hundred dollars a year."

Exhausted, humbled, I at last quitted the warmed Horace Mann ozone for the harsh and searching atmosphere of the street. And I gazed up at the pile, and saw all its interiors again in my mind. I had not grasped the half nor the quarter of what had been so willingly and modestly shown to me. I had formed no theory as to the value of some of the best juvenile education in the Eastern States. But I had learned one thing. I knew the secret of the fine, proud bearing of young America. A child is not a fool; a child is almost always uncannily shrewd. And when it sees a splendid palace provided for it, when it sees money being showered upon hygienic devices for its comfort, even upon trifles for its distraction, when it sees brains all bent on discovering the best, nicest ways of dealing with its instincts, when it sees itself the center of a magnificent pageant, ritual, devotion, almost worship, it naturally lifts its chin, puts its shoulders back, steps out with a spring, and glances down confidently upon the whole world. Who wouldn't?

It was an exciting day for me when I paid a call next door to Horace Mann and visited Columbia University. For this was my first visit of inspection to any university of any kind, either in the New World or in the Old. As for an English university education, destiny had deprived me of its advantages and of its perils. I could not haughtily compare Columbia with Oxford or Cambridge, because I had never set foot even in their towns. I had no standards whatever of comparison.

I arose and went out to lunch on that morning, and left the lunch before anybody else and rushed in an automobile to Columbia; but football had already begun for the day in the campus costing two million dollars, and classes were over. I saw five or more universities while I was in America, but I was not clever enough to catch one of them in the act of instruction. What I did see was the formidable and magnificent machine, the apparatus of learning, supine in repose.

And if the spectacle was no more than a promise, it was a very dazzling promise. No European with any imagination could regard Columbia as other than a miracle. Nearly the whole of the gigantic affair appeared to have been brought into being, physically, in less than twenty years. Building after building, device after device, was dated subsequent to 1893. And to my mind that was just the point of the gigantic affair. Universities in Europe are so old. And there are universities in America which are venerable. A graduate of the most venerable of them told me that Columbia was not "really" a university. Well, it did seem unreal, though not in his sense; it seemed magic. The graduate in question told me that a university could not be created by a stroke of the wand. And yet there staring me in the face was the evidence that a university not merely could be created by a stroke of the wand, but had been. (I am aware of Columbia's theoretic age and of her insistence on it.) The wand is a modern invention; to deny its effective creative faculty is absurd.

EDUCATION AND ART

Of course I know what the graduate meant. I myself, though I had not seen Oxford nor Cambridge, was in truth comparing Columbia with my dream of Oxford and Cambridge, to her disadvantage. I was capable of saying to myself: "All this is terribly new. All this lacks tradition." Criticism fatuous and mischievous, if human! It would be as sapient to imprison the entire youth of a country until it had ceased to commit the offense of being young. Tradition was assuredly not apparent in the atmosphere of Columbia. Moreover, some of her architecture was ugly. On the other hand, some of it was beautiful to the point of nobility. The library, for instance: a building in which no university and no age could feel anything but pride. And far more important than stone or marble was the passionate affection for Columbia which I observed in certain of her sons who had nevertheless known other universities. A passionate affection also perhaps brought into being since 1893, but not to be surpassed in honest fervency and loyalty by influences more venerable!

Columbia was full of piquancies for me. It delighted me that the Dean of Science was also consulting engineer to the university. That was characteristic and fine. And how splendidly unlike Oxford! I liked the complete life-sized railroad locomotive in the engineering-shops, and the Greek custom in the baths; and the students' notion of coziness in the private dens full of shelves, photographs, and disguised beds; and the visibility of the president; and his pronounced views as to the respective merits of New York newspapers; and the eagerness of a young professor of literature in the Faculty Club to defend against my attacks English Professor A. C. Bradley. I do believe that I even liked the singular sight of a Chinaman tabulating from the world's press, in the modern-history laboratory, a history of the world day by day. I can hardly conceive a wilder, more fearfully difficult way of trying to acquire the historical sense than this voyaging through hot, fresh newspapers, nor one more probably destined to failure (I should have liked to see some of the two-monthly résumés which students in this course are obliged to write); but I liked the enterprise and the originality and the daring of the idea; I liked its disdain of tradition. And, after all, is it weirder than the common traditional method?

To the casual visitor, such as myself, unused either to universities or to the vastness of the American scale, Columbia could be little save an enormous and over-whelming incoherence. It so chiefly remains in my mind. But the ingenious humanity running through the whole conception of it was touching and memorable. And although I came away from my visit still perfectly innocent of any broad theory as to ultimate educational values in America, I came away also with a deeper and more reassuring conviction that America was intensely interested in education, and that all that America had to do in order to arrive at real national, racial results was to keep on being intensely interested. When America shall have so far outclassed Europe as to be able to abolish, in university examinations, what New York picturesquely calls "the gumshoe squad" (of course now much more brilliantly organized in America than in

UNIVERSITY BUILDINGS—UNIVERSITY OF PENNSYLVANIA

Europe), then we shall begin to think that, under the stroke of the wand, at least one real national, racial result has been attained!

When I set eyes on the sixty buildings which constitute the visible part of Harvard University, I perceived that, just as Kensington had without knowing it been imitating certain streets of Boston, so certain lost little old English towns that even American tourists have not yet reached had without knowing it been imitating the courts and chimneys and windows and doorways and luscious brickwork of Harvard. Harvard had a very mellow look indeed. No trace of the wand! The European in search of tradition would find it here in bulk. I should doubt whether at Harvard modern history is studied through the daily paper— unless perchance it be in Harvard's own daily paper. The considerableness of Harvard was attested for me by the multiplicity of its press organs. I dare say that Harvard is the only university in the world the offices of whose comic paper are housed in a separate and important building. If there had been a special press-building for Harvard's press, I should have been startled. But when I beheld the mere comic organ in a spacious and costly detached home that some London dailies would envy, I was struck dumb. That sole fact indicated the scale of magnificence at Harvard, and proved that the phenomenon of gold-depreciation has proceeded further at Harvard than at any other public institution in the world.

The etiquette of Harvard is nicely calculated to

heighten the material splendor of the place. Thus it is etiquette for the president, during his term of office, to make a present of a building or so to the university. Now buildings at Harvard have adopted the excellent habit of never costing less than about half a million dollars. It is also etiquette that the gifts to the university from old students shall touch a certain annual sum; they touch it. Withal, there is no architectural ostentation at Harvard. All the buildings are artistically modest; many are beautiful; scarcely one that clashes with the sober and subtle attractiveness of the whole aggregation. Nowhere is the eye offended. One looks upon the crimson façades with the same lenient love as marks one's attitude toward those quaint and lovely English houses (so familiar to American visitors to our isle) that are all picturesqueness and no bath-room. That is the external effect. Assuredly entering some of those storied doorways, one would anticipate inconveniences and what is called "Old World charm" within.

But within one discovers simply naught but the very latest, the very dearest, the very best of everything that is luxurious. I was ushered into a most princely apartment, grandiose in dimensions, superbly furnished and decorated, lighted with rich discretion, heated to a turn. Portraits by John Sargent hung on the vast walls, and a score of other manifestations of art rivaled these in the attention of the stranger. No club in London could match this chamber. It was, I believe, a sort of lounge for the students. Anyhow, a few students were lounging in it; only a few—there was no rush for the privilege.

And the few loungers were really lounging, in the wonderful sinuous postures of youth. They might have been lounging in a railway station or a barn instead of amid portraits by John Sargent.

The squash-racket court was an example of another kind of luxury, very different from the cunning combinations of pictured walls, books, carved wood, and deep-piled carpets, but not less authentic. The dining-hall seating a thousand simultaneously was another. Here I witnessed the laying of dinner-tables by negroes. I noted that the sudden sight of me instantly convinced one negro, engaged in the manipulation of pats of butter, that a fork would be more in keeping with the Harvard tradition than his fingers, and I was humanly glad thus to learn that the secret reality of table-laying is the same in two continents. I saw not the dining of the thousand. In fact, I doubt whether in all I saw one hundred of the six thousand students. They had mysteriously vanished from all the resorts of perfect luxury provided for them. Possibly they were withdrawn into the privacies of the thousands of suites—each containing bedroom, sitting-room, bath-room, and telephone—which I understood are allotted to them for lairs. I left Harvard with a very clear impression of its frank welcoming hospitality and of its extraordinary luxury.

And as I came out of the final portal I happened to meet a student actually carrying his own portmanteau—and rather tugging at it. I regretted this chance. The spectacle clashed, and ought to have been contrary to etiquette. That student should in propriety have been

159

followed by a Nigerian, Liberian, or Senegambian, carrying his portmanteau.

My visits to other universities were about as brief, stirring, suggestive, and incomplete as those to Columbia and Harvard. I repeat that I never actually saw the educational machine in motion. What it seemed to me that I saw in each case was a tremendous mechanical apparatus at rest, a rich, empty frame, an organism waiting for the word that would break its trance. The fault was, of course, wholly mine. I find upon reflection that the universities which I recall with the most sympathy are those in which I had the largest opportunity of listening to the informal talk of the faculty and its wife. I heard some mighty talking upon occasion—and in particular I sat willing at the feet of a president who could mingle limericks and other drollery, the humanities, science, modern linguistics, and economics in a manner which must surely make him historic.

●

Education, like most things except high-class cookery, must be judged by ultimate results; and though it may not be possible to pass any verdict on current educational methods (especially when you do not happen to have even seen them in action), one can to a certain extent assess the values of past education by reference to the demeanor of adults who have been through it. One of the chief aims of education should be to stimulate the great virtue of curiosity. The worst detractors of the American race—and there are some severe ones in New York, London, and Paris!—will not be able to deny that an unusually active curiosity is a marked characteristic of the race. Only they twist that very characteristic into an excuse for still further detraction. They will, for example, point to the "hordes" (a word which they regard as indispensable in this connection) of American tourists who insist on seeing everything of historic or artistic interest that is visible in Europe. The plausible argument is that the mass of such tourists are inferior in intellect and taste to the general level of Europeans who display curiosity about history or art. Which is probably true. But it ought to be remembered by us Europeans (and in sackcloth!) that the mass of us with money to spend on pleasure are utterly indifferent to history and art. The European dilettante goes to the Uffizi and sees a shopkeeper from Milwaukee gazing ignorantly at a masterpiece, and says: "How inferior this shopkeeper from Milwaukee is to me! The American is an inartistic race!" But what about the shopkeeper from Huddersfield or Amiens? The shopkeeper from Huddersfield or Amiens will be flirting about on some entirely banal beach—Scarborough or Trouville—and for all he knows or cares Leonardo da Vinci might have been a cabman; and yet the loveliest things in the world are, relatively speaking, at his door! When the European shopkeeper gets as far as Lucerne in August, he thinks that a journey of twenty-four hours entitles him to rank a little lower than Columbus. It was an enormous feat for him to reach Lucerne, and he must have credit for it, though his interest in art is in no wise thereby demonstrated. One has to admit that he now goes to Lucerne in hordes. Praise be to him! But I imagine that the American horde "hustling for culture" in no matter what historic center will compare pretty favorably with the European horde in such spots as Lucerne.

All general curiosity is, to my mind, righteousness, and I so count it to the American. Not that I think that American curiosity is always the highest form of curiosity, or that it is not limited. With its apparent omnivorousness it is often superficial and too easily satisfied—particularly by mere words. Very seldom is it profound. It is apt to browse agreeably on externals. The American, like Anglo-Saxons generally, rarely shows a passionate and yet honest curiosity about himself or his country, which is curiosity at its finest. He will divide things into pleasant and unpleasant, and his curiosity is trained to stop at the frontier of the latter—an Anglo-Saxon device for being comfortable in your mind! He likes to know what others think of him and his country, but he is not very keen on knowing what he really thinks on these subjects himself. The highest form of curiosity is apt to be painful sometimes. (And yet who that has practised it would give it up?) It also demands intellectual honesty—a quality which has been denied by Heaven to all Anglo-Saxon races, but which nevertheless a proper education ought in the end to achieve. Were I asked whether I saw in America any improvement upon Britain in the supreme matter of intellectual honesty, I should reply, No. I seemed to see in America precisely the same tendency as in Britain to pretend, for the sake of instant comfort, that things are not what they are, the same timid but determined dislike of the whole truth, the same capacity to be shocked by notorious and universal phenomena, the same delusion that a refusal to look at these phenomena is equivalent to the destruction of these phenomena, the same flaccid sentimentality which vitiates practically all Anglo-Saxon art. And I have stood in the streets of New York, as I have stood in the streets of London, and longed with an intense nostalgia for one hour of Paris, where, amid a deplorable decadence, intellectual honesty is widely discoverable, and where absolutely straight thinking and talking is not mistaken for cynicism.

Another test of education is the feeling for art, and the creation of an environment which encourages the increase of artistic talent. (And be it noted in passing that the intellectually honest races, the Latin, have been the most artistic, for the mere reason that intellectual dishonesty is just sentimentality, and sentimentality is the destroying poison of art.) Now the most exacerbating experience that fell to me in America —and it fell more than once—was to hear in discreetly lighted and luxurious drawing-rooms, amid various mural proofs of trained taste, and usually from the lips of an elegantly Europeanized American woman with a sad, agreeable smile: "There is no art in the United States. . . . I feel like an exile." A number of these exiles, each believing himself or herself to be a solitary lamp in the awful darkness, are dotted up and down the great cities, and it is a curious fact that they bitterly despise one another. In so doing they are not very wrong. For, in the first place, these people, like nearly all dilettanti of art, are extremely unreliable judges of racial characteristics. Their mentality is allied to that of the praisers of time past, who, having read *Tom Jones* and *Clarissa*, are incapable of comprehending that the immense majority of novels produced in the eighteenth century were nevertheless terrible rubbish. They go to a foreign land, deliberately confine their attention to the artistic manifestations of that country, and then exclaim in ecstasy: "What an artistic country this is! How different from my own!" To the same class belong certain artistic visitors to the United States who, having in their own country deliberately cut themselves off from intercourse with ordinary inartistic persons, visit America, and, meeting there the average man and woman in bulk, frown superiorly and exclaim: "This Philistine race thinks of nothing but dollars!" They cannot see the yet quite evident truth that the rank and file of every land is about equally inartistic. Modern Italy may in the mass be more lyrical than America, but in either architecture or painting Italy is simply not to be named with America.

Further, and in the second place, these people never did and never will look in the right quarters for vital art. A really original artist struggling under their very noses has small chance of being recognized by them, the reason being that they are imitative, with no real opinion of their own. They associate art with Florentine frames, matinée hats, distant museums, and clever talk full of allusions to the dead. It would not occur to them to search for American art in the architecture of railway stations and the draftsmanship and sketch-

MITCHELL TOWER AND HUTCHINSON COMMONS—UNIVERSITY OF
CHICAGO

writing of newspapers and magazines, because they have not the wit to learn that genuine art flourishes best in the atmosphere of genuine popular demand.

Even so, with all their blindness, it is unnatural that they should not see and take pride in the spectacular historical facts which prove their country to be less negligible in art than they would assert. I do not mean the existence in America of huge and glorious collections of European masters. I have visited some of these collections, and have taken keen pleasure therein. But I perceive in them no national significance—no more national significance than I perceive in the endowment of splendid orchestras to play foreign music under foreign conductors, or in the fashionable crowding of classical concerts. Indeed, it was a somewhat melancholy experience to spend hours in a private palace crammed with artistic loveliness that was apparently beloved and understood, and to hear not one single word disclosing the slightest interest in modern American art. No, as a working artist myself, I was more impressed and reassured by such a sight as the Innes room at the colossal Art Institute of Chicago than by all the collections of old masters in America, though I do not regard Innes as a very distinguished artist. The aforesaid dilettanti would naturally condescend to the Innes room at Chicago's institute, as to the long-sustained, difficult effort which is being made by a school of Chicago sculptors for the monumental ornamentation of Chicago. But the dilettanti have accomplished a wonderful feat of unnaturalness in forgetting that their poor, inartistic Philistine country did provide, *inter alia*, the great writer who has influenced French imaginative writers more deeply than any other foreign writer since Byron —Edgar Allan Poe; did produce one of the world's supreme poets—Whitman; did produce the greatest pure humorist of modern times; did produce the miraculous Henry James; did produce Stanford White and the incomparable McKim; and did produce the only two Anglo-Saxon personalities who in graphic art have been able to impose themselves on modern Europe—Whistler and John Sargent.

In the matter of graphic art, I have known so many American painters in Paris that I was particularly anxious to see what American painting was like at home. My first adventures were not satisfactory. I trudged through enormous exhibitions, and they filled me with just the same feeling of desolation and misery that I experienced at the Royal Academy, London, or the Société des Artistes Français, Paris. In miles of slippery exercise I saw almost nothing that could interest an intelligent amateur who had passed a notable portion of his life in studios. The first modern American painting that arrested me was one by Grover, of Chicago. I remember it with gratitude. Often, especially in New York, I was called upon by stay-at-home dilettanti to admire the work of some shy favorite, and with the best will in the world I could not, on account of his too obvious sentimentality. In Boston I was authoritatively informed that the finest painting in the whole world was at that moment being done by a group of Boston artists in Boston. But as I had no opportunity to see their work, I cannot offer an opinion on the proud claim. My gloom was becoming permanent, when one wet day I invaded, not easily, the Macdowell Club, and, while listening to a chorus rehearsal of Liszt's "St. Elizabeth" made the acquaintance of really interesting pictures by artists such as Irving R. Wiles, Jonas Lie, Henri, Mrs. Johansen, and Brimley, of whom previously I had known nothing. From that moment I progressed. I met the work of James Preston, and of other men who can truly paint.

All these, however, with all their piquant merits, were Parisianized. They could have put up a good show in Paris and emerged from French criticism with dignity. Whereas there is one American painter who has achieved a reputation on the tongues of men in Europe without (it is said) having been influenced by Europe, or even having exhibited there. I mean Winslow Homer. I had often heard of Winslow Homer from connoisseurs who had earned my respect, and assuredly one of my reasons for coming to America was to see Winslow Homer's pictures. My first introduction to his oil-paintings was a shock. I did not like them, and I kept on not liking them. I found them theatrical and violent in conception, rather conventional in design, and repellent in color. I thought the painter's attitude toward sea and rock and sky decidedly sentimental beneath its wilful harshness. And I should have left America with broken hopes of Winslow Homer if an enthusiast for State-patronized art had not insisted on taking me to the State Museum at Indianapolis. In this agreeable and interesting museum there happened to be a tempo-

rary loan exhibit of water-colors by Winslow Homer.
Which water-colors were clearly the productions of a
master. They forced me to reconsider my views of
Homer's work in general. They were beautiful; they
thrilled; they were genuine American; there is nothing
else like them. I shall never forget the pleasure I felt
in unexpectedly encountering these summary and highly
distinguished sketches in the quietude of Indianapolis.
I would have liked to collect a trainful of New York,
Chicago, and Boston dilettanti, and lead them by the
ears to the unpretentious museum at Indianapolis, and
force them to regard fixedly these striking creations.
Not that I should expect appreciation from them!
(Indianapolis, I discovered, was able to keep perfectly
calm in front of the Winslow Homer water-colors.)
But their observations would have been diverting.

VIII

CITIZENS

VIII

NOTHING in New York fascinated me as much as the indications of the vast and multitudinous straitened middle-class life that is lived there; the average, respectable, difficult, struggling existence. I would always regard this medium plane of the social organism with more interest than the upper and lower planes. And in New York the enormity of it becomes spectacular. As I passed in Elevated trains across the end of street after street, and street after street, and saw so many of them just alike, and saw so many similar faces mysteriously peering in the same posture between the same curtains through the same windows of the same great houses; and saw canaries in cages, and enfeebled plants in pots, and bows of ribbon, and glints of picture-frames; and saw crowd after dense crowd fighting down on the cobbled roads for the fearful privilege of entering a surface-car—I had, or seemed to have, a composite vision of the general life of the city.

And what sharpened and stimulated the vision more than anything else was the innumerable flashing glimpses of immense torn clouds of clean linen, or linen almost clean, fluttering and shaking in withdrawn courtyards between rows and rows of humanized windows. This domestic detail, repugnant possibly to some, was particularly impressive to me; it was the visible index of what life really is on a costly rock ruled in all material essentials by trusts, corporations, and the grand principle of tipping.

I would have liked to live this life, for a space, in any one of half a million restricted flats, with not quite enough space, not quite enough air, not quite enough dollars, and a vast deal too much continual strain on the nerves. I would have liked to come to close quarters with it, and yet its subtle and sinister toxin incurably into my system. Could I have done so, could I have participated in the least of the uncountable daily dramas of which the externals are exposed to the gaze of any starer in an Elevated, I should have known what New York truly meant to New-Yorkers, and what was the real immediate effect of average education reacting on average character in average circumstances; and the knowledge would have been precious and exciting beyond all knowledge of the staggering "wonders" of the capital. But, of course, I could not approach so close to reality; the visiting stranger seldom can; he must be content with his imaginative visions.

Now and then I had the good-fortune to come across illuminating stories of New York dailiness, tales of no important event, but which lit up for me the whole expanse of existence in the hinterlands of the Elevated. As, for instance, the following. The tiny young wife of the ambitious and feverish young man is coming home in the winter afternoon. She is forced to take the street-car, and in order to take it she is forced to fight. To fight, physically, is part of the daily round

PART OF THE DAILY ROUND OF THE INDOMITABLE NEW YORK
WOMAN

of the average fragile, pale, indomitable New York woman. In the swaying crowd she turns her head several times, and in tones of ever-increasing politeness requests a huge male animal behind her to refrain from pushing. He does not refrain. Being skilled, as a mariner is skilled in beaching himself and a boat on a surfy shore, she does ultimately achieve the inside of the car, and she sinks down therein apparently exhausted. The huge male animal follows, and as he passes her, infuriated by her indestructible politeness, he sticks his head against her little one and says, threateningly, "What's the matter with you, anyway?" He could crush her like a butterfly, and, moreover, she is about ready to faint. But suddenly, in uncontrollable anger, she lifts that tiny gloved hand and catches the huge male animal a smart smack in the face. "Can't you be polite?" she hisses. Then she drops back, blushing, horrified by what she has done. She sees another man throw the aghast male animal violently out of the car, and then salute her with: "Madam, I take off my hat to you." And the tired car settles down to apathy, for, after all, the incident is in its essence part of the dailiness of New York.

The young wife gets home, obsessed by the fact that she has struck a man in the face in a public vehicle. She is still blushing when she relates the affair in a rush of talk to another young wife in the flat next to hers. "For Heaven's sake don't tell my husband," she implores. "If he knew he'd leave me forever!" And the young husband comes home, after his own personal dose of street-car, preoccupied, fatigued, nervous, hungry,

demanding to be loved. And the young wife has to be-
have as though she had been lounging all the afternoon
in a tea-gown on a soft sofa. Curious that, although
she is afraid of her husband's wrath, the temptation to
tell him grows stronger! Indeed, is it not a rather fine
thing that she has done, and was not the salute of the
admiring male flattering and sweet? Not many tiny
wives would have had the pluck to slap a brute's face.
She tells the young husband. It is an error of tact on
her part. For he, secretly exacerbated, was waiting for
just such an excuse to let himself go. He is angry, he
is outraged—as she had said he would be. What—his
wife, *his*—etc., etc.!

A night full of everything except sleep; full of Elevated and rumbling cars, and trumps of autos, and the
eternal liveliness of the cobbled street, and all incomprehensible noises, and stuffiness, and the sense of other
human beings too close above, too close below, and to
the left and to the right, and before and behind, the
sense that there are too many people on earth! What
New-Yorker does not know the wakings after the febrile
doze that ends such a night? The nerves like taut
strings; love turned into homicidal hatred; and the
radiator damnably tapping, tapping! . . . The young
husband afoot and shaved and inexpensively elegant,
and he is demanding his fried eggs. The young wife is
afoot, too, manœuvering against the conspiracies of the
janitor, who lives far below out of sight, but who per-
meates her small flat like a malignant influence. . . . Hear
the whistling of the dumb-waiter! . . . Eggs are demanded,
authoritatively, bitterly. If glances could kill, not only

that flat but the whole house would be strewn with
corpses. . . . Eggs! . . . .

Something happens, something arrives, something
snaps; a spell is broken and horror is let loose. "Take
your eggs!" cries the tiny wife, in a passion. The eggs
fly across the table, and the front of a man's suit is
ruined. She sits down and fairly weeps, appalled at
herself. Last evening she was punishing males; this
morning she turns eggs into missiles, she a loving, an
ambitious, an intensely respectable young wife! As for
him, he sits motionless, silent, decorated with the colors
of eggs, a graduate of a famous university. Calamity
has brought him also to his senses. Still weeping, she
puts on her hat and jacket. "Where are you going?"
he asks, solemnly, no longer homicidal, no longer hungry.
"I must hurry to the cleaners for your other suit!" says
she, tragic. And she hurries. . . .

A shocking story, a sordid story, you say. Not a
bit! They are young; they have the incomparable
virtue of youthfulness. It is naught, all that! The
point of the story is that it illustrates New York—a
New York more authentic than the spaciousness of
upper Fifth Avenue or the unnatural dailiness of grand
hotels. I like it.

You may see that couple later in a suburban house—
a real home for the time being, with a colorable imitation of a garden all about it, and the "finest suburban
railway service in the world": the whole being a
frame and environment for the rearing of children. I

have sat at dinner in such houses, and the talk was of nothing but children; and anybody who possessed any children, or any reliable knowledge of the ways of children, was sure of a respectable hearing and warm interest. If one said, "By the way, I think I may have a photograph of the kid in my pocket," every eye would reply immediately: "Out with it, man—or woman!—and don't pretend you don't always carry the photograph with you on purpose to show it off!" In such a house it is proved that children are unmatched as an exhaustless subject of conversation. And the conversation is rendered more thrilling by the sense of partially tamed children—children fully aware of their supremacy—prowling to and fro unseen in muddy boots and torn pinafores, and speculating in their realistic way upon the mysteriousness of adults.

"We are keen on children here," says the youngish father, frankly. He is altered now from the man he was when he inhabited a diminutive flat in the full swirl of New York. His face is calmer, milder, more benevolent, and more resignedly worried. And assuredly no one would recognize in him the youth who howled murderously at university football matches and cried with monstrous ferocity at sight of danger from the opposing colors: "Kill him! Kill him for me! I can't stand his red stockings coming up the field!" Yet it is the same man. And this father, too, is the fruit of university education; and further, one feels that his passion for his progeny is one of the chief causes of American interest in education. He and his like are at the root of the modern university—not the millionaires. In Chicago

CITIZENS

I was charmed to hear it stoutly and even challengingly maintained that the root of Chicago University was not Mr. Rockefeller, but the parents of Chicago.

Assuming that the couple have no children, there is a good chance of catching them later, splendidly miserable, in a high-class apartment-house, where the entire daily adventure of living is taken out of your hands and done for you, and you pay a heavy price in order to be deprived of one of the main interests of existence. The apartment-house ranks in my opinion among the more pernicious influences in American life. As an institution it is unhappily establishing itself in England, and in England it is terrible. I doubt if it is less terrible in its native land. It is anti-social because it works always against the preservation of the family unit, and because it is unfair to children, and because it prevents the full flowering of an individuality. (Nobody can be himself in an apartment-house; if he tried that game he would instantly be thrown out.) It is immoral because it fosters bribery and because it is pretentious itself and encourages pretense in its victims. It is unfavorable to the growth of taste because its decorations and furniture are and must be ugly; they descend to the artistic standard of the vulgarest people in it, and have not even the merit of being the expression of any individuality at all. It is enervating because it favors the creation of a race that can do absolutely nothing for itself. It is unhealthy because it is sometimes less clean than it seems, and because often it forces its victims to eat in a dining-room whose walls are a distressing panorama of Swiss scenery, and because its cuisine is and must be

at best mediocre, since meals at once sound and showy
cannot be prepared wholesale.

Some apartment-houses are better than others; many
are possibly marvels of organization and value for money.
But none can wholly escape the indictment. The institution itself, though it may well be a natural and inevitable by-product of racial evolution, is bad. An
experienced dweller in apartment-houses said to me, of
a seeming-magnificent house which I had visited and
sampled: "We pay six hundred dollars for two poor
little rooms and a bath-room, and twenty-five dollars
a week for board, whether we eat or not. The food is
very bad. It is all kept hot for about an hour, on steam,
so that every dish tastes of laundry. Everything is an
extra. Telephone—lights—tips—especially tips. I tip
everybody. I even tip the *chef*. I tip the *chef* so that,
when I am utterly sick of his fanciness and prefer a mere
chop or a steak, he will choose me an eatable chop or
steak. And that's how things go on!"

My true and candid friend, the experienced dweller
in apartment-houses, was, I have good reason to believe,
an honorable man. And it is therefore a considerable
tribute to the malefic influence of apartment-house life
that he had no suspicion of the gross anti-social im-
morality of his act in tipping the *chef*. Clearly it was an
act calculated to undermine the *chef's* virtue. If all the
other experienced dwellers did the same, it was also
a silly act, producing no good effect at all. But if only
a few of them did it, then it was an act which resulted
in the remainder of the victims being deprived of their
full, fair chance of getting eatable chops or steaks. My

friend's proper course was obviously to have kicked up
a row, and to have kicked up a row in a fashion so clever
that the management would not put him into the street.
He ought to have organized a committee of protest, he
ought to have convened meetings for the outlet of public
opinion, he ought to have persevered day after day and
evening after evening, until the management had been
forced to exclude uneatable chops and steaks utterly
from their palatial premises and to exact the honest
performance of duty from each and all of the staff. In
the end it would have dawned upon the management
that inedible food was just as much out of place in the
restaurant as counterfeit bills and coins at the cash-
desk. The proper course would have been difficult and
tiresome. The proper course often is. My friend took
the easy, wicked course. That is to say, he exhibited
a complete lack of public spirit.

An apartment-house is only an apartment-house;
whereas the republic is the republic. And yet I permit
myself to think that the one may conceivably be the
mirror of the other. And I do positively think that
American education does not altogether succeed in the
very important business of inculcating public spirit
into young citizens. I judge merely by results. Most
peoples fail in the high quality of public spirit; and the
American perhaps not more so than the rest. Perhaps
all I ought to say is that according to my own limited
observation public spirit is not among the shining attri-
butes of the United States citizen. And even to that
statement there will be animated demur. For have not

the citizens of the United States been conspicuous for their public spirit? . . .

It depends on what is meant by public spirit—that is, public spirit in its finer forms. I know what I do *not* mean by public spirit. I was talking once to a member of an important and highly cultivated social community, and he startled me by remarking:

"The major vices do not exist in this community at all."

I was prepared to credit that such Commandments as the Second and Sixth were not broken in that community. But I really had doubts about some others, such as the Seventh and Tenth. However, he assured me that such transgressions were unknown.

"What do you *do* here?" I asked.

He replied: "We live for social service—for each other."

The spirit characterizing that community would never be described by me as public spirit. I should fit it with a word which will occur at once to every reader.

On the other hand, I cannot admit as proof of public spirit the prevalent American habit of giving to the public that which is useless to oneself—no matter how immense the quantity given, and no matter how admirable the end in view. When you have got the money it is rather easy to sit down and write a check for five million dollars, and so bring a vast public institution into being. It is still easier to leave the same sum by testament. These feats are an affair of five minutes or so; they cost simply nothing in time or comfort or peace of mind. If they are illustrations of public spirit, it is a low and facile form of public spirit.

CITIZENS

True public spirit is equally difficult for the millionaire and for the clerk. It is, in fact, very tedious work. It implies the quiet daily determination to get eatable chops and steaks by honest means, chiefly for oneself, but incidentally for everybody else. It necessitates trouble and inconvenience. I was in a suburban house one night, and it was the last night for registering names on an official list of voters before an election; it was also a rainy night. The master of the house awaited a carriage, which was to be sent up by a candidate, at the candidate's expense, to take him to the place of registration. Time grew short.

"Shall you walk there if the carriage doesn't come?" I asked, and gazed firmly at the prospective voter.

At that moment the carriage came. We drove forth together, and in a cabin warmed by a stove and full of the steam of mackintoshes I saw an interesting part of the American Constitution at work—four hatted gentlemen writing simultaneously the same particulars in four similar ledgers, while exhorting a fifth to keep the stove alight. An acquaintance came in who had trudged one mile through the rain. That acquaintance showed public spirit. In the ideal community a candidate for election will not send round carriages in order, at the last moment, to induce citizens to register; in the ideal community citizens will regard such an attention as in the nature of an insult.

I was told that millionaires and presidents of trusts were chiefly responsible for any backwardness of public spirit in the United States. I had heard and read the same thing about the United States in England. I was

therefore curious to meet these alleged sinister creatures.
And once, at a repast, I encountered quite a bunch of
millionaire-presidents. I had them on my right hand
and on my left. No two were in the least alike. In
my simplicity I had expected a type—formidable, in-
timidating. One bubbled with jollity; obviously he
"had not a care in the world." Another was grave. I
talked with the latter, but not easily. He was taciturn.
Or he may have been feeling his way. Or he may have
been not quite himself. Even millionaire-presidents
must be self-conscious. Just as a notorious author is
too often rendered uneasy by the consciousness of his
notoriety, so even a millionaire-president may sometimes have a difficulty in being quite natural. However, he did ultimately talk. It became clear to me that
he was an extremely wise and sagacious man. The lines
of his mouth were ruthlessly firm, yet he showed a general sympathy with all classes of society, and he met my
radicalism quite half-way. On woman's suffrage he was
very fair-minded. As to his own work, he said to me
that when a New York paper asked him to go and be
cross-examined by its editorial board he willingly went,
because he had nothing to conceal. He convinced me
of his uprightness and of his benevolence. He showed
a nice regard for the claims of the Republic, and a proper
appreciation of what true public spirit is.

Some time afterward I was talking to a very prominent New York editor, and the conversation turned to
millionaires, whereupon for about half an hour the editor agreeably recounted circumstantial stories of the
turpitude of celebrated millionaires—stories which he

alleged to be authentic and undeniable in every detail. I had to gasp. "But surely—" I exclaimed, and mentioned the man who had so favorably impressed me.

"Well," said the editor, reluctantly, after a pause, "I admit he has *the new sense of right and wrong* to a greater extent than any of his rivals."

I italicize the heart of the phrase, because it is italicized in my memory. No words that I heard in the United States more profoundly struck me. Yet the editor had used them quite ingenuously, unaware that he was saying anything singular! . . . Since when is the sense of right and wrong "new" in America?

Perhaps all that the editor meant was that public spirit in its higher forms was growing in the United States, and beginning to show itself spectacularly here and there in the immense drama of commercial and industrial policies. That public spirit is growing, I believe. It chanced that I found the basis of my belief more in Chicago than anywhere else.

❧

I have hitherto said nothing of the "folk"—the great mass of the nation, who live chiefly by the exercise, in one way or another, of muscular power or adroitness, and who, if they possess drawing-rooms, do not sit in them. Like most writers, when I have used such phrases as "the American people" I have meant that small dominant minority which has the same social code as myself. Goethe asserted that the folk were the only real people. I do not agree with him, for I have never found one city more real than another city, nor one class of people more real than another class. Still, he was

Goethe, and the folk, though mysterious, are very real; and, since they constitute perhaps five-sixths of the nation, it would be singular to ignore them. I had two brief glimpses of them, and the almost theatrical contrast of these two glimpses may throw further light upon the question just discussed.

I evaded Niagara and the Chicago Stock-yards, but I did not evade the "East Side" of New York. The East Side insisted on being seen, and I was not unwilling. In charge of a highly erudite newspaper man, and of an amiable Jewish detective, who, originally discovered by Colonel Roosevelt, had come out first among eighteen hundred competitors in a physical examination, my particular friend and I went forth one intemperate night to "do" the East Side in an automobile. We saw the garlanded and mirrored core of "Sharkey's" saloon, of which the most interesting phenomenon was a male pianist who would play the piano without stopping till 2.30 A.M. With about two thousand other persons, we had the privilege of shaking hands with Sharkey. We saw another saloon, frequented by murderers who resembled shop assistants. We saw a Hebraic theater, whose hospitable proprietor informed us how he had discovered a great play-writing genius, and how on the previous Saturday night he had turned away seven thousand patrons for lack of room! Certainly on our night the house was crammed; and the play seemed of realistic quality, and the actresses effulgently lovely. We saw a Polack dancing-hall, where the cook-girls were slatterns, but romantic slatterns. We saw Seward Park, which is the dormitory of the East Side in summer.

CITIZENS

We saw a van clattering off with prisoners to the night court. We saw illustrious burglars, "gunmen," and "dukes" of famous streets—for we had but to raise a beckoning finger, and they approached us, grinning, out of gloomy shadows. (And very ordinary they seemed in spite of slashed faces!)

We even saw Chinatown, and the wagonettes of tourists stationary in its streets. I had suspected that Chinatown was largely a show for tourists. When I asked how it existed, I was told that the two thousand Chinese of Chinatown lived on the ten thousand Chinese who came into it from all quarters on Sundays, and I understood. As a show it lacked convincingness—except the delicatessen-shop, whose sights and odors silenced criticism. It had the further disadvantage, by reason of its tawdry appeals of color and light, of making one feel like a tourist. Above a certain level of culture, no man who is a tourist has the intellectual honesty to admit to himself that he is a tourist. Such honesty is found only on the lower levels. The detective saved our pride from time to time by introducing us to sights which the despicable ordinary tourists cannot see. It was a proud moment for us when we assisted at a conspiratorial interview between our detective and the "captain of the precincts." And it was a proud moment when in an inconceivable retreat we were permitted to talk with an aged Chinese actor and view his collection of flowery hats. It was a still prouder (and also a subtly humiliating) moment when we were led through courtyards and beheld in their cloistral aloofness the American legitimate wives of wealthy China-

185

men, sitting gorgeous, with the quiescence of odalisques, in gorgeous uncurtained interiors. I was glad when one of the ladies defied the detective by abruptly swishing down her blind.

But these affairs did not deeply stir my imagination. More engaging was the detective's own habit of stopping the automobile every hundred yards or so in order to point out the exact spot on which a murder, or several murders, had been committed. Murder was his chief interest. I noticed the same trait in many newspaper men, who would sit and tell excellent murder stories by the hour. But murder was so common on the East Side that it became for me curiously puerile—a sort of naughtiness whose punishment, to be effective, ought to wound, rather than flatter, the vanity of the child-minded murderers. More engaging still was the extraordinary frequency of banks—some with opulent illuminated signs—and of cinematograph shows. In the East End of London or of Paris banks are assuredly not a feature of the landscape—and for good reason. The cinematograph is possibly, on the whole, a civilizing agent; it might easily be the most powerful force on the East Side. I met the gentleman who "controlled" all the cinematographs, and was reputed to make a million dollars a year net therefrom. He did not appear to be a bit weighed down, either by the hugeness of his opportunity or by the awfulness of his responsibility.

The supreme sensation of the East Side is the sensation of its astounding populousness. The most populous street in the world—Rivington Street—is a sight not to be forgotten. Compared to this, an up-town thor-

THE ASTOUNDING POPULOUSNESS OF THE EAST SIDE

oughfare of crowded middle-class flats is the open country—is an uninhabited desert! The architecture seemed to sweat humanity at every window and door. The roadways were often impassable. The thought of the hidden interiors was terrifying. Indeed, the hidden interiors would not bear thinking about. The fancy shunned them—a problem not to be settled by sudden municipal edicts, but only by the efflux of generations. Confronted by this spectacle of sickly-faced immortal creatures, who lie closer than any other wild animals would lie; who live picturesque, feverish, and appalling existences; who amuse themselves, who enrich themselves, who very often lift themselves out of the swarming warren and leave it forever, but whose daily experience in the warren is merely and simply horrible —confronted by this incomparable and overwhelming phantasmagoria (for such it seems), one is foolishly apt to protest, to inveigh, to accuse. The answer to futile animadversions was in my particular friend's query: "Well, what are you going to do about it?"

My second glimpse of the folk was at quite another end of the city of New York—namely, the Bronx. I was urgently invited to go and see how the folk lived in the Bronx; and, feeling convinced that a place with a name so remarkable must itself be remarkable, I went. The center of the Bronx is a racket of Elevated, bordered by banks, theaters, and other places of amusement. As a spectacle it is decent, inspiring confidence but not awe, and being rather repellent to the sense of beauty. Nobody could call it impressive. Yet I departed from the

Bronx very considerably impressed. It is the interiors of the Bronx homes that are impressive. I was led to a part of the Bronx where five years previously there had been six families, and where there are now over two thousand families This was newest New York.

No obstacle impeded my invasion of the domestic privacies of the Bronx. The mistresses of flats showed me round everything with politeness and with obvious satisfaction. A stout lady, whose husband was either an artisan or a clerk, I forget which, inducted me into a flat of four rooms, of which the rent was twenty-six dollars a month. She enjoyed the advantages of central heating, gas, and electricity; and among the landlord's fixtures were a refrigerator, a kitchen range, a bookcase, and a sideboard. Such amenities for the people—for the *petits gens*—simply do not exist in Europe; they do not even exist for the wealthy in Europe. But there was also the telephone, the house exchange being in charge of the janitor's daughter—a pleasing occupant of the entrance-hall. I was told that the telephone, with a "nickel" call, increased the occupancy of the Bronx flats by ten per cent.

Thence I visited the flat of a doctor—a practitioner who would be the equivalent of a "shilling" doctor in a similar quarter of London. Here were seven rooms, at a rent of forty-five dollars a month, and no end of conveniences—certainly many more than in any flat that I had ever occupied myself! I visited another house and saw similar interiors. And now I began to be struck by the splendor and the cleanliness of the halls, landings, and staircases: marble halls, tesselated landings, and stairs out of Holland; the whole producing a gorgeous effect—to match the glory of the embroidered pillow-cases in the bedrooms. On the roofs were drying-grounds, upon which each tenant had her rightful "day," so that altercations might not arise. I saw an empty flat. The professional vermin exterminator had just gone—for the landlord-company took no chances in this detail of management.

Then I was lifted a little higher in the social-financial scale, to a building of which the entrance-hall reminded me of the foyers of grand hotels. A superb negro held dominion therein, but not over the telephone girl, who ran the exchange ten hours a day for twenty-five dollars a month, which, considering that the janitor received sixty-five dollars and his rooms, seemed to me to be somewhat insufficient. In this house the corridors were broader, and to the conveniences was added a mail-shoot, a device which is still regarded in Europe as the final word of plutocratic luxury rampant. The rents ran to forty-eight dollars a month for six rooms. In this house I was asked by hospitable tenants whether I was not myself, and, when I had admitted that I was myself, books of which I had been guilty were produced, and I was called upon to sign them.

The fittings and decorations of all these flats were artistically vulgar, just as they are in flats costing a thousand dollars a month, but they were well executed, and resulted in a general harmonious effect of innocent prosperity. The people whom I met showed no trace of the influence of those older artistic civilizations whose charm seems subtly to pervade the internationalism of the East Side. In certain strata and streaks of society on the East Side things artistic and intellectual are comprehended with an intensity of emotion and understanding impossible to Anglo-Saxons. This I know.

The Bronx is different. The Bronx is beginning again, at a stage earlier than art, and beginning better. It is a place for those who have learnt that physical righteousness has got to be the basis of all future progress. It is a place to which the fit will be attracted, and where the fit will survive. It has rather a harsh quality. It reminded me of a phrase used by an American at the head of an enormous business. He had been explaining to me how he tried a man in one department, and, if he did not shine in that, then in another, and in another, and so on. "And if you find in the end that he's honest but not efficient?" I asked. "Then," was the answer, "we think he's entitled to die, and we fire him."

The Bronx presented itself to me as a place where the right of the inefficient to expire would be cheerfully recognized. The district that I inspected was certainly, as I say, for the fit. Efficiency in physical essentials was inculcated—and practised—by the landlord-company, whose constant aim seemed to be to screw up higher and higher the self-respect of its tenants. That the landlord-company was not a band of philanthropists, but a capitalistic group in search of dividends, I would readily admit. But that it should find its profit in the business of improving the standard of existence and appealing to the pride of the folk was to me a wondrous sign of the essential vigor of American civilization, and a proof that public spirit, unostentatious as a coral insect, must after all have long been at work somewhere.

Compare the East Side with the Bronx fully, and one may see, perhaps roughly, a symbol of what is going forward in America. Nothing, I should imagine, could be more interesting to a sociological observer than that actual creation of a city of homes as I saw it in the Bronx. I saw the home complete, and I saw the home incomplete, with wall-papers not on, with the roof not on. Why, I even saw, further out, the ground being leveled and the solid rock drilled where now, most probably, actual homes are inhabited and babies have been born! And I saw further than that. Nailed against a fine and ancient tree, in the midst of a desolate waste, I saw a board with these words: "A new Subway station will be erected on this corner." There are legendary people who have eyes to see the grass growing. I have seen New York growing. It was a hopeful sight, too.

At this point my impressions of America come to an end, for the present. Were I to assert, in the phrase conventionally proper to such an occasion, that no one can be more sensible than myself of the manifold defects, omissions, inexactitudes, gross errors, and general lack of perspective which my narrative exhibits, I should assert the thing which is not. I have not the slightest doubt that a considerable number of persons are more sensible than myself of my shortcomings; for on the subject of America I do not even know enough to be fully aware of my own ignorance. Still, I am fairly sensible of the enormous imperfection and rashness of this book. When I regard the map and see the trifling extent of the ground that I covered—a scrap tucked away in the northeast corner of the vast multi-colored territory—I marvel at the assurance I displayed in choosing my title. Indeed, I have yet to see your United States. Any Englishman visiting the country for the second time, having begun with New York, ought to go round the world and enter by San Francisco, seeing Seattle before Baltimore and Denver before Chicago. His perspective might thus be corrected in a natural manner, and the process would in various ways be salutary. It is a nice question how many of the opinions formed on the first visit—and especially the most convinced and positive opinions—would survive the ordeal of the second.

As for these brief chapters, I hereby announce that I am not prepared ultimately to stand by any single view which they put forward. There is naught in them which is not liable to be recanted. The one possible justification of them is that they offer to the reader the one thing that, in the very nature of the case, a mature and accustomed observer could not offer—namely, an immediate account (as accurate as I could make it) of the first tremendous impact of the United States on a mind receptive and unprejudiced. The greatest social historian, the most conscientious writer, could not recapture the sensations of that first impact after further intercourse had scattered them.

THE END